D0753932

TRAGEDIES
OF THE
CROWSNEST PASS

The Crowsnest Pass on the Alberta-B.C. border has experienced almost every conceivable type of disaster from a deadly shoot-out to an RCAF plane crash on Ptolemy Mountain which killed seven airmen. Over 600 people have died in fires, explosions, floods, avalanches and other calamities.
The photo above shows some of the 128 dead miners arriving at Fernie from the 1902 explosion at Coal Creek.

THE COVERS

FRONT: The Frank Slide and the
Alberta Government's excellent Frank Slide Interpretive
Centre. (Latter photo courtesy Alberta Culture.)

BACK: In a grave nearly 200 feet long at Hillcrest lie 150 of the miners. They were
buried in two rows, as far as possible relative beside relative, buddy beside buddy.
Although it was June, a blustery west wind blew swirling snow through
the cemetery.

PHOTO CREDITS

B.C. Provincial Archives: 74-75, 78, 80, 82; Glenbow Archives: 6, 10, 11, 14,
18, 24, 30, 34, 36-37, 41, 44, 56, 66; Heritage House: front and back covers,
inside back cover, 91, 93; Provincial Archives of Alberta: 3, 4-5, 47, 49, 52-53,
57, 60-61, 68-69; Travel Alberta: inside back cover (centre); Tourism B.C.:
inside front cover; Vern Decoux: 86-87.

CANADIAN CATALOGUING IN PUBLICATION DATA

Main entry under title:

Tragedies of the Crowsnest Pass

Contents: The Crowsnest, pass of tragedy — The Frank slide / by Frank Anderson
— Hillcrest Mine disaster / by Frank Anderson — Fernie, city under a curse / by
Elsie G. Turnbull — The Crowsnest Pass today.
ISBN 0-919214-58-4

1. Crowsnest Pass (Alta. and B.C.) — History. 2. Disasters — Crowsnest Pass
(Alta. and B.C.) — History. I. Anderson, Frank W., 1919-   II. Turnbull, Elsie
G. (Elsie Grant), 1903-   Fernie, city under a curse.
FC3695.C76T73 1984   971.23'4   C84-091054-1
F1079.C76T73 1984

Copyright © 1983 Heritage House Publishing Company Ltd.
Published in 1983. Reprinted in 1985, 1992.

All rights reserved. No part of this publication may be reproduced, stored in a retrieval system,
or transmitted in any form or by any means, electronic, mechanical, photocopying, recording or
otherwise, without the prior written permission of Heritage House Publishing Company Ltd.

Heritage House Publishing Company Ltd.
Box 1228, Station A
Surrey, B.C. V3S 2B3

Printed in Canada

George Rudeychuk, a coal miner typical of thousands who worked in the Crowsnest Pass in the early 1900s.

CONTENTS

THE CROWSNEST: PASS OF TRAGEDY

The Crowsnest Pass is about sixty miles long, straddling the southern Alberta-B.C. border in the Canadian Rockies. Probably nowhere else in Canada has so much tragedy occurred in so few miles. In disasters from avalanches to town-consuming forest fires, rock slides to mine explosions, over 600 men, women and children have been burned alive, crushed by boulders, and blown apart by explosions.

The coal mines have experienced the worst disasters. In the miles of

Miners and their horses at Hillcrest. Coal mines in the Alberta-B.C. section of the Crowsnest Pass have claimed over 500 lives.

underground tunnels over 500 men died in searing explosions of coal dust or deadly gas known as "blackdamp."

Coal was first noted on the Elk River in 1845 by Father Jean de Smet, a missionary who worked with the Kootenay Indians in what is today southern British Columbia and northern Montana. In a letter he wrote that he had seen large pieces of coal along the river and that "I am convinced that this fossil could be abundantly procured." His words were prophetic since the region would prove to contain some of the world's largest coal reserves.

Discovery of the Crowsnest Pass by white men is credited to Michael Phillips. He was an Englishman who arrived in the area in 1864 to work as a clerk for the Hudson's Bay Company. In 1870 he left the firm and started a ranch and sawmill near present Roosville. At the same time he

trapped and prospected, following to their headwaters many of the tributaries of the area's two main rivers, the Elk and the Flathead.

In 1873 with John Collins and four pack horses he left on another prospecting and trapping trip up the Elk River. Instead of gold, however, they were disappointed to find nothing but coal. As Phillips later wrote, "... formation of the country was promising for coal but very discouraging for the gold hunter."

After they reached a creek named Michel for an Indian chief they continued exploring eastward. A few days later they were astonished to find large trails which were not made by elk, the main wildlife of the region. Then they noticed that the trees were covered with buffalo hair. Phillips later wrote: "... it was evident to both of us that we had passed through the Rocky Mountains without going over any range. This is the first trip ever made by what is now known as the Crow's Nest Pass."

The next year Phillips with three companions returned to the Elk River area to explore further. One creek they found they named Morrissey after Jim Morrissey, one of the group. All were disappointed, however, as there was only coal, no traces of gold. On the next creek coal was even more abundant. They named it Coal Creek, for as Phillips noted, "We could find nothing but coal and coal everywhere."

Despite this disappointment, Phillips still had faith in the country. Of the route he and trapper John Collins had discovered through the Rockies he wrote: "I saw the advantage of a pass through a great rocky range without a mountain to go over and I determined to work for a trail."

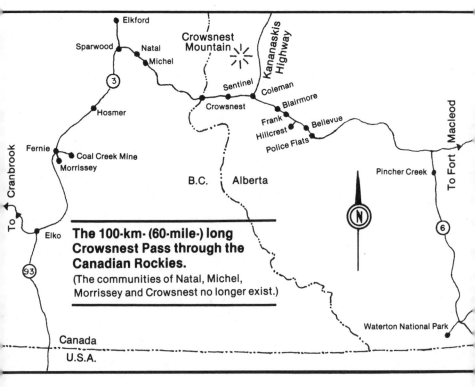

The 100-km- (60-mile-) long Crowsnest Pass through the Canadian Rockies.

(The communities of Natal, Michel, Morrissey and Crowsnest no longer exist.)

A main obstacle proved to be the British Columbia government's representative in the area, Gold Commissioner William Fernie. "The Indians say there was no such pass," he stated, "and there is no use wasting the money."

Phillips persisted, however, and was given permission to hire one man and blaze a trail through the Pass. In 1879 it was completed. Two years later the Canadian Pacific Railway explored the area as a possible route for its trans-continental line. But the Canadian government opposed the route "for military reasons." In other words, the government felt it was too close to the U.S. border. The Rogers Pass to the north subsequently became the route of Canada's first coast-to-coast rail link.

The year after the railway explorers left the Crowsnest, Dr. George M. Dawson of the Geological Survey of Canada documented additional coal outcroppings. Apart from heating the homes of a few isolated settlers, however, the coal had no commercial value. There was no viable means of getting it to market.

Railway promoters were well aware of the problem — and the potential for profit. As a consequence between 1884-1896 many firms expressed a desire to lay steel in exchange for cash subsidies, land grants and other benefits. All these proposals were doomed. The Federal government's policy was that the project was too important from a national viewpoint to be exploited by short-term speculators.

As a result in June 1897 "The Crowsnest Pass Agreement" became law. Under it the Canadian Pacific Railway through a subsidiary, The British Columbia Southern, would construct a branch from its main line near Medicine Hat through the Crowsnest Pass to Kootenay Lake in British Columbia.

The company moved rapidly, with first contracts awarded in July. Since the Crowsnest Pass is among the lowest in the Rockies and fairly wide there were none of the massive problems encountered in building the main line through Rogers Pass to the north. Here over 200 workmen had died in avalanches, and huge snowsheds had to be built to prevent trains being swept into valleys. (See Heritage House book, *Incredible Rogers Pass*.) By autumn 1898 the British Columbia Southern was complete.

With the arrival of the railway major companies began developing the massive outcroppings which flanked the Pass for some forty-five miles of its sixty-mile length. (One gigantic seam in British Columbia was found to be 180 feet thick, with parts believed to be 600 or more feet thick.) In addition to being plentiful, the coal proved excellent for turning into coke to power the railway engines.

Development of mines was rapid, with communities quickly appearing to serve them. On the Alberta side Blairmore was the first, born in 1898. Soon there were ten communities in fourteen miles, with producing mines at Passburg, Bellevue, Hillcrest, Frank, Lille, Blairmore and Coleman. Across the border in B.C. there were mines at Natal, Michel, Morrissey, Hosmer and Coal Creek (Fernie).

While the millions of tons of coal pouring from the mine tipples created prosperity, extracting it resulted in dreadful disasters engulfing virtually every community. In most of the mines flanking the Pass the coal contained large quantities of methane gas and the mining methods created clouds of coal dust.

It was a lethal combination since the methane gas was highly inflammable; the coal dust, highly explosive. A methane gas fire usually resulted in a cataclysmic coal-dust explosion. Even more deadly than the explosion was the "blackdamp" or "afterdamp," — carbon dioxide left after an explosion had burned the oxygen from the air. Scores of miners who survived devastating underground blasts were killed by the carbon dioxide. Death in the mines became so common that the Federal Department of Mines and Minerals for nearly fifty years issued statistics showing the number of tons of coal mined per serious injury and fatality.

The first explosion occurred in the International Mine at Coleman, about three miles west of Blairmore, on April 3, 1907. All those underground survived the blast but three miners died from the afterdamp. Coleman's second explosion was at the McGillivray Mine in 1926. Ten miners died. The blast fortunately occurred on the night shift when few men were working. Had it occurred on the day shift, the death toll could have been twenty or thirty times higher. As it was the mine caught fire and had to be flooded. It was months before grieving relatives could bury their sons, husbands and fathers.

Three miles east of Blairmore another mining community, Bellevue, had its first — and only — disaster on December 9, 1910. Thirty miners died in an explosion south of the town. Residents were horror stricken at the disaster, little knowing it soon would be dreadfully overshadowed.

On the morning of June 19, 1914, 228 miners left their homes at Bellevue's neighboring community of Hillcrest and climbed to the Hillcrest Mine. It was considered the safest mine in the area, operating for nine years with no serious accidents. Tragically, at 9:30 that Friday morning something triggered a fire in the methane gas. It skipped along the roof of the mine shaft until it encountered a pocket of coal dust. There was a massive explosion, followed by killing afterdamp. Of the 228 miners who went underground that morning, 189 died in Canada's worst mine disaster. Virtually every family in Hillcrest was affected. Some 130 women were left without a husband and 400 children without a father. The dead men were buried in three graves, the largest 200 feet long containing 150 bodies in two rows.

The mine re-opened and operated death-free until September 19, 1926. That afternoon some 150 men were making final preparations to start their night shift. In the mine were only two men — fireboss Frank Lote and Fred Jones who was attending the pumping system. There was a sudden thunderous explosion. Rescuers found both men dead and evidence that the blast was more devastating than the one in 1914 which took 189 lives. Had it occurred two hours later 150 men would have been in the tunnels. Most could have perished.

These numbers of disasters have been almost equalled on the B.C. side of the Crowsnest Pass. At the now abandoned community of Crowsnest near the B.C.-Alberta border there is a cemetery which contains some thirty graves. They are believed to be construction workers who died in 1898 of typhoid fever.

The worst mine disaster in the B.C. portion of the Crowsnest Pass was on May 22, 1902, at Coal Creek — today called Fernie. That day an explosion in No. 2 mine still ranks with the greatest coal mine catastrophes in Canada. One hundred and twenty-eight miners died.

There were to be additional tragedies at the Coal Creek mine. In an explosion in 1917 another thirty-four miners died; in 1928 six more were killed and in 1935 an additional three died in a "bump," or underground movement of the earth. In all, the mine took over 160 lives.

Fernie, however, has had tragedies in addition to its mine disasters. In 1904 a fire wiped out the community's entire business section. No lives were lost but the next fire was different. It started on August 1, 1908. Except for a small group of buildings separated from the main town by lawns, the fire destroyed everything in the community of 5,000. Ten people died and losses were a then astronomical $5 million.

Other communities wracked by fires and explosions were Michel-Natal, about halfway through the Pass. In 1904 seven men died in an explosion which also set Michel on fire and destroyed half of it. While the cause was never ascertained, a careless workman was believed responsible.

On August 8, 1916, a mysterious blast occurred in No. 3 mine near the eastern entrance to Natal. The blast occurred during a thunderstorm and killed twelve men. No satisfactory reason was uncovered. Lightning was considered a possible cause but the theory rejected.

At Michel on July 15, 1938, an explosion rocked No. 3 mine, also during a thunderstorm. The mine was idle that day, a lucky circumstance for those on the regular shift. Unfortunately, of five maintenance men inside only two survived. This time the cause was unmistakable. Lightning had struck the mine rails and caused the killer explosion deep inside the tunnel. The steel rails were grounded and another potential hazard was defused, although at least fifteen men had died before the deadly hazard was identified.

The last in the Crowsnest Pass mine disasters that in less than forty years had killed over 500 miners occurred at Michel on April 3, 1967. The afternoon shift of thirty-two men entered North Palmer Mine operated by Crow's Nest Industries Limited. A few minutes later an explosion — or series of explosions — turned the tunnels into a tomb. Fifteen miners died — nearly fifty per cent of those who had gone underground a few minutes before.

But mining disasters and engulfing fires have not been the only tragedies of the Crowsnest Pass. Over the years five police officers were shot to death. One robber died in a shoot-out and three others were hanged — one a woman. At Coal Creek (Fernie) in 1912 a massive snow and rock slide killed six men. The biggest slide, however, had occurred a few years previously on the Alberta side of the Pass. In 1903 some 90 million tons of rock sheered off Turtle Mountain and engulfed part of the town of Frank. At least seventy-six men, women and children died, most while asleep.

In all, over 600 have died in various tragedies in the Crowsnest Pass. On the following pages are descriptions of the three worst. They shattered the communities of Frank, Hillcrest and Fernie.

THE FRANK SLIDE

It was late afternoon, April 28, 1903. Raoul Green took his eyes from the transit sight and squinted at the sun sinking into the V between Turtle and Goat Mountains at the west end of the Crowsnest Pass. Five-thirty, he estimated, then checked his pocket watch as a matter of formality.

"It's five-thirty. Time to wrap it up," he called to his assistant who was already moving the level to a new location. The boy telescoped the level and joined him.

"Where do you want to hide the equipment tonight, Mr. Green?"

The surveyor glanced around at the bush and rocks, trying to decide

Frank, the ill-fated community at the foot of Turtle Mountain.

upon a hiding place for their expensive instruments. Rather than pack the heavy equipment two miles back to Blairmore every night, they had been in the habit of concealing it in the underbrush, ready for service the next morning. He had almost chosen a suitable place when he stopped suddenly — he had a strange feeling.

Raoul Green's gaze moved from the valley to the mist-hidden crest of Turtle Mountain, towering 3,000 feet above them. A swirling grey mass of cloud was strung along the mountain top like an untidy tablecloth. "We'll take it back to the hotel tonight," he decided abruptly.

"But, Mr. Green, we always leave it . . . ." The lad groaned at the thought of the two-mile hike along the railroad tracks to Blairmore.

"I know," Green answered, picking up the delicate transit. "But I've got a funny feeling. Tonight we're taking it back."

As they scrambled down the embankment onto the roadbed of the Canadian Pacific Railway, Green could not help glancing apprehensively at the mist which hid a series of massive rolls of limestone that jutted outward above the valley. There was no real reason for his concern. It was true an old Indian legend that the mountain moved was talked about by the ranchers and trappers, and discouraged the Indians from camping at its base, but there had never been any indication that it was unsafe.

As the two men trudged westward along the tracks, they passed McVeigh and Poupore's construction camp — a dozen tents pitched on the right-of-way between the railway and Turtle Mountain. On their right the valley rose sharply northwards and the mining town of Lille, six miles away. The West Canadian Collieries had opened coal properties at Lille the previous year and constructed the Frank and Grassy Mountain Railway on a gradual but rather steep grade down from Lille to just north of Frank. J.J. Leutot, manager, had decided to extend this spur along the valley and join the CPR about a mile east of Frank where six coke ovens had been built. McVeigh and Poupore had completed the main section of the line the previous October and were now waiting to begin work on the connecting link.

Directly behind the construction camp the ground sloped gently towards the Oldman River which flowed eastward through the Crowsnest Pass and along the base of Turtle Mountain. Ahead and slightly to the left of the CPR sprawled Frank itself, separated from the rest of the valley by Gold Creek which joined the Oldman under the shadow of the mountain.

Frank, North-West Territories — the region did not become part of the new province of Alberta until 1905 — owed its existence to coal which Henry S. Pelletier had discovered outcropping on Turtle Mountain in 1900. He sold his claim to Samuel W. Gebo, a promoter who had already established mining operations near Burmis, a small community to the east. Gebo, backed by H.L. Frank of Butte, Montana, developed the find in the spring of 1901. The mine entrance was opened about 30 feet above the river level and a spur line built from the CPR tracks. On the flats west of Gold Creek the company constructed twenty-five cottages, a large boarding house for single miners, and office buildings for their operation.

The nearest town with hotel accommodation was Blairmore, two miles to the west, which expected to enjoy a boom with the opening of the Frank mines. Owing to a land dispute among some of the original settlers at Blairmore, however, businessmen were reluctant to establish there. They looked to the Canadian American Coal Company for leadership, and Frank and Gebo acted promptly to attract business to their embryo village. With a flair for showmanship, the two entrepreneurs decided that their venture should begin with a gala opening of the townsite on September 10, 1901.

On the day of the reception, the CPR ran two special trains — one from Lethbridge, the other from Cranbrook to the west in British

Columbia. The local newspapers in the area carried feature stories on the event, headlining the fact that the only expense would be rail fare, the rest was free. H.L. Frank missed his own train connection but in true flamboyant style hired an engine and caboose and overtook the eastbound special at Moyie, B.C. When he arrived at Frank, nearly 1,400 spectators were swarming over the flats.

In a lavish ceremony that saw Sir Fred Haultain, Premier of the North-West Territories and Sir Clifford Sifton, Minister of the Interior in the Laurier government, making proud speeches that everyone promptly forgot, the little mining community was launched. Following the formal opening, there was a lacrosse game between Lethbridge and Fernie and a football game between Blairmore and Pincher Creek. There were footraces and sporting events with gold medals for the winners. Then the guests sat down to a lavish dinner in the open, for which a ton of fresh fruit and ice cream had been brought from Spokane. There were tours of the company cottages, designed to attract the more stable, married coal miner. There were even tours of the mine itself which had already penetrated into Turtle Mountain for 1,250 feet.

When the day was over and the trains had gone, there was more than one miner, more than one businessman, who had been impressed with the possibilities of the new community. Among them was a young Scot, Alexander Leitch, who had left his family at Oak Lake, Manitoba, to explore the business prospects of the Crowsnest Pass.

With an objective of 1,000 tons of coal a day, the mine began to forge ahead, sometimes recklessly ignoring safety rules and sound mining practice. By the spring of 1903 the miners had penetrated over 5,000 feet, ripping out seams of coal that varied from 9 to 12 feet wide. Frank now had a population nearing 600, served by an electric light plant, waterworks system and two-story school. In addition there were four hotels and some sixteen other business establishments along a booming main thoroughfare called Dominion Avenue. Business lots sold from $400 to $600 apiece, while residential lots brought $250.

On that April 23 night that Raoul Green and his assistant trudged along the railway tracks, the community was well on its way to prosperity and stability. Emphasizing the latter points was the laughter that Green and his assistant heard as spectators encouraged the local ball team at practice for its first game of the season. Green left the equipment in his room at the Alberta Hotel in Blairmore and went to the dining room for supper. It was 6 p.m. Much of Frank and upwards of 100 residents had only a few hours left to live.

In Frank, Ellen Thornley washed the last supper dish and set it on the shelf above the kitchen sink. In the front room of the house, which also served as a shoe shop, she could hear her brother, John, bidding goodnight to the last customer. She went outside to empty the dishwater and when she returned her brother was waiting. "Ellen, what say we stay at the hotel tonight. Your train comes in early tomorrow."

"But it's still the same distance to walk," protested Ellen with a laugh.

"Oh, I was just thinking that it would be fun to spend your last night

Frank in 1902, showing rows of miners' cottages. The slide buried houses under rocks up to 100 feet deep. Buildings which survived, below at far right, were sheltered by the unbroken section of Turtle Mountain.

in Frank at a wicked hotel," he joked. "In any case, you wouldn't have to rush like mad in the morning."

Ellen agreed. She had just completed treatment for rheumatism at the Sulphur Springs Sanatorium at Frank and had planned to spend her last night quietly with her brother. But on John's whim she went cheerfully into the bedroom to pack.

As they left the shoe shop and walked towards town, they could hear the cheers from the ball game. They stopped to talk with friends and acquaintances enjoying the last of the lovely spring day. The rough footpath brought them to the livery stable which housed some fifty horses used in dray work and in the mine. Robert Watt, the stable boss, and his assistant, Francis Rochette, were just completing the chores before going uptown. Next door was a small log cabin occupied by Alfred "Jack" Dawe and two friends from Wales. They passed the temporary clapboard house of William Warrington, a miner from Macdonald's Corners in Ontario. The Warringtons had three teenage children and staying with them Alex Dixon, a friend from their home town. Near the Warringtons was another clapboard house where lived six miners from Lancashire, England. No one knew much about them except that they were bachelors.

Once past the houses, the path led by a row of miners' cottages, then veered and crossed a wooden bridge over Gold Creek before zig-zagging through a clearing dotted with rocks and jackpine stumps. At the edge of the clearing the path joined Dominion Avenue, the main business thoroughfare.

With its wooden sidewalks, dirt road, hitching racks and false-front buildings, Dominion Avenue resembled a scene from the Old West. D.J. McIntyre's hall boasted a good stage and piano and opened for concerts, theatricals, lodge meetings, dances and Church services. Farther along the street, Marks and Buchanan operated Crown Studios, a sign in the window boasting "Our photographs will always whisper, Come Again." There were two restaurants — the Palm which advertised "Meals at all Hours," and the Frank Cafe. Genial Harry Matheson, a groom of only four months, published the *Frank Sentinel* from his tiny newspaper office on Dominion Avenue. While the first issue had greeted the community on October 12, 1901, neither time nor practice had improved the editor's spelling or his stock of type.

At the top of the street, near the site of the new CPR station still under construction, was the Union Bank of Canada. On mine paydays the bank reportedly paid out upwards of $125,000 in American silver dollars. The bank manager, J.H. Farmer, obviously a man of caution, was reputed to have kept four loaded revolvers in his apartment above the bank. Beyond, Alex Leitch's Grocery and Furniture Store ran stiff competition to the Albert Mercantile Company Store. The Post Office was at the end of the street.

Despite its frontier appearance, Frank offered most of the luxuries of the day. A.V. Lang operated a ladies ready-to-wear clothing store, while F. Thompson and J.J. Murphy catered to the men. Suits at Murphy's ranged from $11 to $20, with the proprietor advising that it was "No trouble to show goods." H. Gibead with his Wines, Brandies and

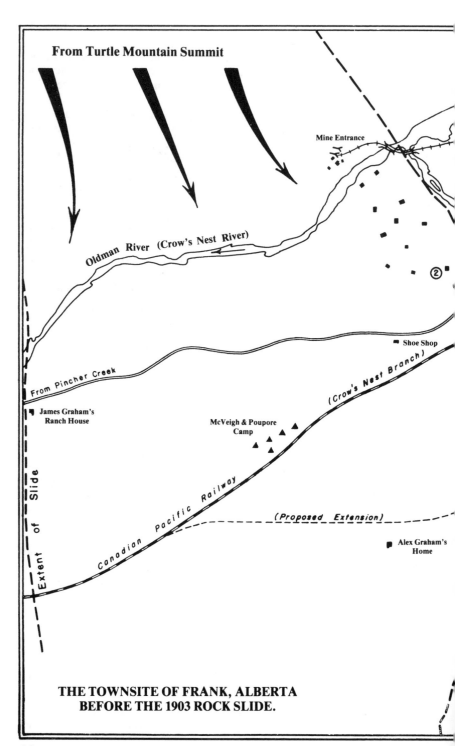

From Turtle Mountain Summit

Mine Entrance

Oldman River (Crow's Nest River)

②

Shoe Shop

From Pincher Creek

(Crow's Nest Branch)

James Graham's
Ranch House

McVeigh & Poupore
Camp

Extent of Slide

Canadian Pacific Railway

(Proposed Extension)

Alex Graham's
Home

**THE TOWNSITE OF FRANK, ALBERTA
BEFORE THE 1903 ROCK SLIDE.**

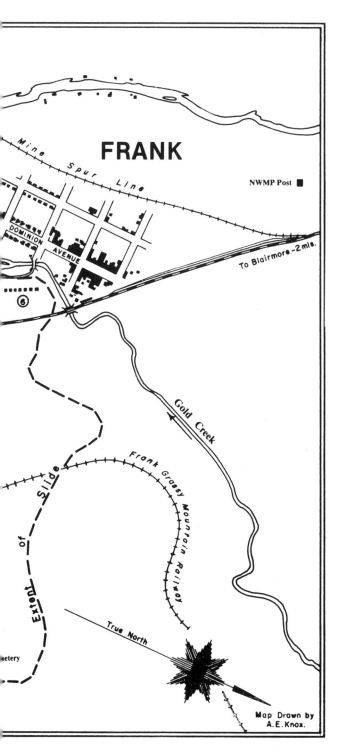

FRANK

NWMP Post ■

1   Boarding House.
2   Lancashire Miners.
3   W. Warrington.
4   Livery Stable
5   Dawe Cabin.
6   Miners' Houses.

Mine Spur Line

DOMINION AVENUE

To Blairmore -2 mls.

Gold Creek

Frank Grassy Mountain Railway

Extent of Slide

Cemetery

True North

Map Drawn by
A.E.Knox.

Whiskeys Store catered to the liquid needs of Frank, while on the next street Minister D.G. McPhail of Knox Presbyterian Church strove to combat the evils of Demon Rum. Those getting married could get a licence from watchmaker Alex Cameron, bring their children into the world with the services of Doctors G.H. Malcolmson or Tom O'Hagan and purchase milk "furnished from one cow" from J.S. Carter's Frank Dairy. Dr. W. Barratt Clayton fixed teeth, S.J. Beebe's Union Laundry supplied diapers, and K.M. Langdon insured the lives of Frank's townspeople. For disagreements there was even a barrister, T.B. Martin.

Travellers could stay at the Imperial Hotel which boasted "The best $2.00 a day house in Alberta" with steam heat, electric light and plaster throughout. To get plastered inside, one had only to visit the bar. There were three other hotels — the Frank, the Union and the Miners.

It was the Frank Hotel that Ellen and John Thornley checked into at 6:30 p.m. Like its competitors, the hotel was already preparing for the nightly sessions of drinking, blackjack and poker.

Meanwhile, John McVeigh, general manager of the McVeigh and Poupore construction camp, left the office tent and walked slowly towards the horse corral at the east end of the camp. He found Jack Leonard, stable boss for the outfit, at the corral. "Quite a mist over the Turtle tonight," McVeigh observed, nodding to the towering cliffs above.

"Yeah, can't see much of Gebo's lonely mountain," Leonard quipped. "Are the extra men and horses coming in Friday?"

"Yes. I think you should head over to Pincher Creek and buy more hay. The survey is just about completed and the Breckenridge and Lund crew will be joining us. We'll need plenty of hay for their teams."

Jack Leonard reached for his saddle and bridle. "In that case, I'd better get going before it's too dark to see the trail."

John McVeigh waited for his assistant to saddle up and saw him on the thirty-mile ride before retracing his steps. On the way he checked with Joe Britton, a two-fisted brawler who was labor foreman. There were only a dozen laborers in camp that night, a skeleton crew of taciturn men who could not write their names — or preferred not to. Bookkeeper J.J. Scott listed them on the records as The Banton Kid, Olaf, the Swede or some similar concealing name. As McVeigh talked with Britton the men were coming from their tents, walking down the tracks towards Frank to sample the wares of the Imperial, Union or Frank hotels. Sometime after midnight they would swagger back along the ties, in varying degrees of sobriety, richer or poorer from playing the cards, but all ready for a night's rest before another day of toil. Next day they would be joined by about 130 men from the Breckenridge and Lund Construction Company who would move in to help with the last link of the Frank and Grassy Mountain Railway.

McVeigh walked back to the office tent, noting that already the chill of the night was setting in, crisping the ground which had thawed with the exceptionally warm weather of the past few days. Normally, he would have returned to the Alberta Hotel in Blairmore where he lived with his wife and child, but they had gone to visit her parents near Calgary. His brother, P. McVeigh, and partner, J. Poupore, would normally have been with him but they were away on business in Macleod. With a last look at the almost deserted camp, McVeigh went inside and drew the flaps.

FATE IS THE HUNTER

North-West Mounted Police Constable Robert Bruce Leard checked his uniform and equipment before stepping out into the crisp night air for his evening tour of duty. In his early twenties, Leard had been transferred to Frank in the fall of 1902. Together with his superior, Corporal Jack Allan who was at Macleod on a case, Leard was responsible for keeping order in the community. His self-inspection completed, Leard briskly walked the half mile to Frank, conscious that the night was getting colder.

He slowed to a stroll as he reached his beat along Dominion Avenue, his leather heels clacking sharply. Though noise from the hotel bars would have convinced a stranger that mayhem was being committed every minute, Leard ignored it. It was still early in the evening. At the end of Dominion he found the footpath to the eastern flats and followed it over the wooden bridge to the row of miners' cottages — all brightly lit except the vacant one at the end of the row.

The Bansemers lived in the first house, closest to town. Carl, a native of Germany, had first settled in Nova Scotia but the prospect of work in the West had brought him and his family to the Crowsnest Pass. While the black coal of the mine gave a living to the Bansemers, their real ambition was for a homestead. Shortly after arriving at Frank they had located one near Lundbreck, a hamlet to the east. Earlier that day, Carl and his two

Only the bravery of brakeman Sid Choquette prevented the *Spokane Flyer* from slamming into the miles of rubble left by the slide.

eldest sons, Rufus and Henry, had left for the homestead with a load of furniture. His wife, Annie, with their remaining seven children, remained at home.

As Leard passed the second house, he could hear Rosemary Leitch playing the piano. Originally from the Ottawa Valley, she and her husband, Alex, had been lured by the glamor of the West. They had made their first stop at Oak Lake, Manitoba, in the 1880s. In partnership with his three brothers, Alex had tried the flour-milling business but in 1901 came West and decided to settle at Blairmore. The land dispute at Blairmore, however, and the opening of Frank with its promise of prosperity brought him to the mining town. Not content with the cramped company cottage for his wife and seven children, Leitch had enlarged the kitchen and added a second bedroom for the boys. The family was one of the most respected in the community, active in church work and popular as guests.

The next house was occupied by Charles Ackroyd, a miner from Montana, with his wife and thirteen-year-old stepson, Lester Johnson. Like many other families in Frank, the Ackroyds had known tragedy. His wife had been born in Wisconsin and married a home town lad. Of their family of thirteen, ten died in a smallpox epidemic and in 1891 her husband was killed in a mine accident. She raised the three remaining children — Ida, Charles, and Lester — working to support them until her marriage to Ackroyd. With the discovery of coal and the opening of the Frank mines, Ackroyd had joined the northward stream of miners into Crowsnest Pass, bringing Lester with him.

Their neighbors in the fourth red and white house were the Sam Ennis family. As well as working in the mine, Sam drove the coal dray delivering coal to the villagers. Besides himself and his wife, there were two boys and two girls, all under ten. Living with them was James Warrington, a brother of Mrs. Ennis who also worked in the mine. James was notable because of a black mustache of truly magnificent proportions that was the pride of the family and the envy of local young bloods.

John Watkins lived with his wife and three teen-age children in the fifth cottage. Like the majority of Frank's residents, Watkins had gravitated to Frank with the bad times. Of the children, Thomas could look forward to a life of coal mining, while the two girls, Fernie and Ruby, would probably marry miners and worry about cave-ins and explosions.

The sixth cottage was vacant and in the seventh and last the lights were already going out. Alex Clark, a miner on the night shift, was in the habit of catching a nap before he left for the mine. His eldest daughter, Lillian, would soon be returning from work in the mine boarding house, whose lights could be seen just across Gold Creek. The rest of his children — Charles, Albert, Alfred, Ellen and Gertrude whose ages ranged from five to fifteen — were already in bed.

Constable Leard paused when he arrived at this last cottage in the row. To his left, night was already reaching down to cover Tallon Peak and Goat Mountain. In the far distance beyond the railway track he could make out the lights of Alexander Graham's ranch house. The valley to the north was quiet. From the right the river rushed musically through its rocky banks and the occasional sound of clanking mine machinery at the tipple across the stream reached Leard's ears. Between him and the base of the mountain were about ten temporary dwellings. Although the coal company discouraged shack building, the rapid expansion of the village demanded emergency accommodation.

Among these temporary dwellings was William Warrington's home and its neighboring cottage where the six Lancashire miners lived. Beyond them in the darkness were the residences of Ben Cunes, George Williams, Dan Mitchell, and James Vandusen, who had arrived at Frank only a fortnight before. Originally intending to ranch on the prairie, Vandusen had heard of the building boom in Frank and decided to continue his trade as a carpenter before embarking on his plans to start a dairy farm.

In all, some fifty people lived in the valley beyond Gold Creek and between the railway and the river. Destiny, finances and wanderlust had led them across the world, pausing here, moving there. Regardless, fate had decreed that each would rendezvous with death at the base of Turtle Mountain.

Constable Leard continued his beat, passing between the livery stable and the log cabin occupied by Dawe and his Welsh miners. Leard had no inkling of the danger lurking above. Although the Indians talked about the "mountain that walked" there had never been any indication that it was unstable. A favorite pastime of the miners had been climbing Turtle Mountain for its panoramic view of the countryside. This night was like many another, with no wind through the Pass and a sky hidden in darkness. There was only the sound of rushing water, the metallic clinking from the mine entrance, and the distant murmur from Dominion Avenue.

At the railway tracks, Leard turned back towards town. The camp watchman was not in sight, but the boxcar of dynamite that was to be used for blasting the last link of the Frank and Grassy Mountain line stood apart on its siding, a safe distance from the town and camp.

Back in town, Leard patrolled the main street until the bulk of the miners, merchants and girls had departed from the hotel bars. By midnight, the last of the construction campworkers had returned to camp and the village was quiet except for the remaining few alcoholics and patient barkeeps. Leard walked back to the log cabin that served as office, jail and barracks and went to bed.

Lillian Clark also went to bed, but not at home. Although she had never spent a night away from home in her life, she worked so late at the boarding house that her fellow workers persuaded her not to return to her mother and brothers and sisters across Gold Creek. By such a quirk of fate her life was to be spared.

Thomas Delap heard a dog howling as he worked in the electric light plant beside the river. He had only a month or so before brought his bride to Frank and would have preferred to have been at the hotel with her. But lips however red have to be fed, and his job entailed night work.

In the cabin beside the coal company livery stable, Alfred "Jack" Dawe stirred in his sleep, cursing his terrier for disturbing the night. Across the room, he heard the measured breathing of his two friends. They should all have been travelling eastward over the CPR tracks to catch a boat for Wales, but a snarl-up in ticket reservations had forced them to cancel their trip for one week more. Reservations or not, however, they intended to leave Frank by the end of the week.

In the Union Hotel, Charles and Robert Chestnut slept soundly. Had fate — and sailing reservations — decreed otherwise, they would have been sleeping in the log cabin by the stable. Instead they had been forced to remain in the hotel until the three Welshmen vacated it.

The night of April 28 became the morning of the 29th as the clock in the Graham's kitchen ticked a measured second. Ned Morgan watched the minute hand creep beyond the midnight mark and rose to leave. It had been a profitable day, selling a cow and a calf to his rancher neighbor.

"Won't you stay the night, Ned?" Mrs. Graham suggested. "We've plenty of room in the house."

"Thank you kindly, Mrs. Graham, but I've left my team down near the village," Morgan replied. "I'd better be getting back to them."

James Graham accompanied Morgan to the yard and took a last look round as his visitor departed. Here, nestled against the foot of Turtle Mountain, bordered by the Oldman River on the left, the CPR on the right, and the indistinct boundary of the village to the west, lay his dream — a dairy farm. With Frank growing steadily and only one other serious competitor, it had seemed wise to locate in the valley. He could have picked any of a dozen choice sites, including one selected by farmer Alex Graham, although no relation, near the cemetery. But he had preferred to settle by the river where he was content, especially since his two sons, John and Joseph, who had served in South Africa during the Boer War had returned unharmed.

Graham's only near neighbor at his river-front location was Andy Grissack, a gnarled old trapper who camped in a tent beside the Oldman winter and summer. He was a great favorite with the children because of his stories — some said greatly exaggerated — of the Lost Lemon Mine and hidden mountain trails. As Ned Morgan's footsteps faded, Graham checked the bunkhouse where Graham's two hired boys called Johnson slept. As his own sons worked in the mine, the Johnsons looked after his growing herd. Both were asleep.

Soon Graham was also, the ranch house an indistinguishable shape against the inky blackness of Turtle Mountain. Neither the ranch house, its occupants, nor the old trapper were to see dawn break.

NINETY MILLION TONS OF ROCK

At midnight a quiet cluster of men began to assemble on the main street of Frank and greeted each other with the monosyllabic grunts of men facing night work. Alex Tashigan, the weigh-scale man, huddled in his sheepskin. At least he wouldn't have to go deep into the belly of the Turtle since his work kept him on the mine tipple all night. Joseph Chapman, a veteran miner and foreman of the night crew, waited impatiently for his gang to assemble. His diminutive assistant, Evan "Halfpint" Jones, leaned against the office building.

They were soon joined by the men from across Gold Creek — John Watkins, William Warrington and Alex Clark. Then Shorty Dawson, Dan

McKenzie, Alex McPhail and Alex Grant came out of the shadows to huddle in the chill air waiting for the others. Talkative Charlie Farrell swung into sight and finally the twentieth and last crew member shuffled out of the darkness.

Chapman checked them and led the way towards the mine tipple. Although he was ostensibly foreman of the night crew, in effect each man knew his job and needed no supervision. They crossed the mine bridge over the Oldman River and made their way up the gentle slope to the entrance.

About the same time Robert Lloyd Watt and Les Ferguson came out of the Imperial Hotel and stretched their legs and backs after a session of blackjack. "I'll walk you back to the bridge, Bob," Ferguson said. "On second thought, why don't you stay with me at the hotel tonight?"

"Thanks, Les, but I think I'll turn in at the stable. See you tomorrow."

They parted on the sidewalk of Frank — Les Ferguson to return to his hotel room, Robert Watt to cross the fateful boundary line of Gold Creek into the eastern flats.

Perhaps as he walked, Robert Watt thought of his children in Lanark, Ontario. At eighteen, he had met and married Mary Ann Macdonald, a young widow with two children. With the smoke of the Riel Rebellion of 1885 still darkening the sky, the Watts had settled on a homestead in Manitoba to raise cows, grain and children. Before her death in 1902, Mary had borne him seven children, six of whom survived her and were living in the East. Eleven years of trying to wrest a living from the poor soil on their homestead had become less attractive and in 1896 the Watts returned to Lanark.

On Mary's death, Robert had been forced to seek work wherever it was to be found. When a job as mine carpenter and stable boss at Frank came to his attention, he snapped it up, leaving his children with relatives. If the job proved steady, he planned to send for his children. Watt checked the barn and looked in on his assistant, Francis Rochette, before climbing the stairs to his own sleeping quarters.

Meanwhile, an extra freight train from Macleod was puffing slowly up the steep grade from Passburg to Frank, slowing from its customary speed of 25 m.p.h. to a laboring 10. At the throttle, veteran engineer Ben Murgatroyd scanned the darkness, alert to any danger. The Crowsnest Pass run was notorious for its broken rails, snow slides and other pranks of nature which could quickly derail the clumsy Mogul engines. Fireman Bud Lahey stoked the ravenous boiler between checking the water gauge.

In the caboose Conductor Henri Pettit checked his train orders. They were far behind schedule because of a snowstorm just outside Macleod and still had a lot of work to do, including picking up coal cars at Frank and a bridge pile-driver. Above him in the gondola, caps tilted over sleepy eyes, brakemen Sid Choquette and Bill Lowes rode the jolting seats with the practised relaxation of long-time railway men.

When they reached the boxcar which served as station at Frank, Conductor Pettit checked with the local agent, T.B. Smith. The *Spokane Flyer,* crack passenger train that shuttled between Lethbridge and

The Alex Clark family in 1893. By 1903 the family included five children. Only Lillian, at right, survived because she was at work.

Although upright, the Bansemer house, below, was badly damaged and moved several feet. The men in front of it are standing on the rubble which buried the Clark house, killing Mrs. Alex Clark and her four children. Her husband also died, killed when the slide demolished the mine tipple.

Spokane, was running an hour and a half behind schedule, also delayed by the snowstorm. It was time-tabled to reach Frank about 4:30 that morning, and the freight would have to lie over on the siding until it passed.

After spotting the train on the siding, Pettit sent the engine and crew to the mine to pick up the coal cars. Then he parked his feet beside the pot-bellied stove in the station and listened to the intermittent clatter of the telegraph key.

At the mine tipple Sid Choquette and his companion hooked up the coal cars, then momentarily chatted with Tashigan, the weigh-scale man, and Fred Farrington and Alex Clark, two miners who had come out of the mine entrance for their 4 a.m. lunches. Just below, in the darkness beside the river, they could see the lights of the boiler-house where engineer Thomas Delap tended the power plant. Beyond the river, the valley was in total darkness. To the left, they could see the lights of hotels in Frank where clerks were already waking guests who would be travelling west on the *Spokane Flyer*.

After hooking the coal cars and the pile-driver to their train, Ben Murgatroyd and his crew switched onto the mine spur again and backed up to the tipple to spot a solitary coal car. Tashigan and the two miners were still eating their lunches.

Thankful that their chore was nearly at an end, Choquette set the brakes of the coal car and pulled the connecting pin between the car and the engine. The Mogul began to roll slowly forward down the incline towards the mine bridge. Choquette and his fellow brakeman, Lowes, trotted alongside the slow moving engine, flapping their arms against the intruding cold.

Far above, a huge rock shivered, fell forward and bounded down the heavily wooded mountain. Then another toppled, impelled by some unseen force. Then another, and another.

Murgatroyd, veteran of more than one close call on the treacherous mountain run, took no chances. Screaming a warning to the walking men, he rammed the throttle home and the Mogul churned forward on its metal wheels. Choquette and Lowes sprinted for the handrails and clung hard while the engine picked up speed on the grade.

Engineer Murgatroyd's quick action saved all their lives. There was a horrendous sound high above them, like a mighty clap of thunder. Ninety million tons of rock broke away from Turtle Mountain. As it plummetted down the precipitous slope, a blast of freezing air raced before it.

Like a screaming juggernaut, the rock careened down the mountain side. It swept over the mine entrance, erasing it entirely, then crashed against the mine tipple and hurled Clark, Farrington and Tashigan into eternity. It caught the blacksmith shop and the solitary railway car and flung them two miles across the valley, twisting the mine spur tracks like threads of silk. Seconds after the racing engine and its horrified crew cleared the bridge, the rocks hit one end of the wooden superstructure. Icy water sprayed high into the air as the bridge swung sideways, then subsided into the river. By then, however, the massive avalanche of rocks was already far across the eastern flats.

Ahead of the deadly rock fall, a solid wall of air toppled the flimsy houses, shacks and tents and hurled men, women and children hundreds of yards. Those asleep had no time to waken. Those awake never knew what was happening. Behind the wind came the churning, grinding mass of rocks which made the night unbelievable with noise and streaks of fire as massive boulders leaped and clashed with each other.

The power plant was obliterated in an instant and the seething mass hurtled onto the valley floor, splaying like a fan. The main stream of rocks shot ahead, smashing the remains of the temporary dwellings, cascading over the livery stable and the Dawes cabin, the construction camp and the boxcar of dynamite before expending itself over the farm of Alex Graham and the cemetery. Another spur shot eastward, cascading over the James Graham dairy farm, the bunkhouse and the two-story farmhouse, burying the buildings with all occupants 100 feet deep. At the same time, another spur followed with almost fanatical precision the east bank of Gold Creek. It pushed an icy wall of grey mud ahead of it and sent it crashing against the row of miners' cottages on the outskirts of Frank. A 500-ton boulder jumped the creek and spun to rest within the village itself.

One hundred seconds after its plunge, the cataclysm of rocks had ploughed across the valley and 500 feet up the opposite slope beyond the tracks. Over the scene, a swirling mass of grey dust hung like a shroud.

It was 4:10 a.m., April 29, 1903.

Joseph Dobeck, who was oiling engines in the train shed 600 feet from the disaster, felt the earth shake and heard the monstrous noise. He stepped outside and peered eastward but could see nothing in the darkness. With a shrug, he returned to his job.

"Mormon Bill," a well known local character, was standing on the street in front of the Miners Hotel, cooling off after a strenuous night of poker. He was rocked on his feet by the blast of wind and heard the din. In less than two minutes all was still. Although all around him men and women were rushing into the streets in their night attire, Bill pulled himself together, attributed the sensations to too much liquor and went home to his shack to sleep soundly.

John Anderson, a more sedate and methodical man who had gone to bed at a respectable hour, was awakened by a hurricane wind that shook his house from shingles to sub-cellar. Bounding to the window he saw a few feet away what he thought was a cloud of smoke cascading past his house. Unaware that the smoke was actually a hurtling sea of limestone, Anderson waited until the din ceased. Then he returned to bed, unaware that in the morning he would look through the same window in utter disbelief.

At the same time, Ellen Thornley was thrown from her bed at the Frank Hotel and unceremoniously dumped on the opposite side of the room as the building rocked from the gigantic force. When she regained her composure, she dressed hurriedly and ran downstairs to find the street in confusion. People were crying that the end of the world had come, others ran from the direction of the unearthly burst of noise. A woman carrying a small child, both in night clothes, ran towards her. Ellen whipped off her heavy coat and wrapped it around them. With hurried thanks, the woman and child fled, away from Gold Creek and the eastern flats.

One hundred miles north near Cochrane, two young men who had just taken their girl friends home after a dance reined in their team. Both had heard what they thought was the sharp report of a giant rifle being fired in the mountains to the south. They checked their watches. It was 4:10 a.m. "Somebody must be having a real party down there," one joked, as he stirred the horses into a trot.

Constable Leard, startled out of sleep by the reverberations, raced to the station. He questioned some of the people milling in the street but no one knew what had occurred. That there must have been an explosion of gigantic proportions at the mine was the most obvious answer. Leard's first thought, knowing the scanty resources of the village, was to call for help from outside.

He found the train crew stunned. Even then, though they had escaped by the length of a bridge, Engineer Murgatroyd and his men had no idea of the magnitude of the catastrophe that had almost engulfed them. That something unusual had occurred could be determined by the rumbling rocks and trembling earth, but darkness shielded the extent of the disaster.

Even as Leard arrived at the station the two brakemen, Choquette and Lowes, were setting out across the rocks to flag down the *Spokane Flyer,* expected within twenty minutes. After learning that the east telegraph line had gone dead, Leard started the wires humming towards Cranbrook in British Columbia, the first major town west of Frank.

Unaware of the magnitude of the slide, Choquette and Lowes plunged into the massive mound of rocks, some still hot from their 3,000-foot skip down the mountain. Their trainman lanterns were little use against the darkness, now mixed with a cloud of grey dust. In astonishment they groped their way around rocks so huge they couldn't see the top. Lowes, short of breath, gave up but Choquette scrambled on, growing more aware that this was no ordinary rockslide. When it seemed that the slide would never end, Choquette found himself on its eastern edge, right where the eastbound tracks emerged from the slide.

A few minutes later, clothes and shoes scarred, breath labored, Choquette flagged down the *Spokane Flyer* as it rolled through the darkness. His action saved another possible disaster. If the train had slammed into the slide more lives could have been lost. Both he and Lowes risked their lives since neither knew if a second rock fall would follow the one that had almost been their memorial.

DEATH AND DESTRUCTION

George Bond, a traveller from Ottawa, was in bed at the Union Hotel when the hurricane wind hit the frame structure. The hotel was violently shaken and seemed to writhe on its foundation. When the movement subsided, Bond leaped into his clothing and ran downstairs. Already lights were going on in homes and people dazedly emerging onto the streets.

Once outside, Bond noticed that a fire had started about 600 feet to the east, across Gold Creek. In company with others, he raced towards it, conscious that somewhere ahead was the sound of rocks tumbling down a mountainside. Since the bridge over the creek had been knocked askew by a wall of mud, he and his companions had to wade the stream. Through the dust-laden air they saw the ruins of several houses, two of which were burning.

A tongue of mud and rocks had broken away from the main body of the slide and played a deadly game of chance with the dwellings. At the extreme eastern end, the cottage of Alex Clark had vanished completely with his wife and five children. The Watkins home was a broken hulk of shattered timbers and boards; the Ennis residence, once a proud red and white cottage, lay in ruins; the Ackroyd home was crushed and burning; the Leitch house, sliced in two at the eaves, was almost demolished, the top half having been carried by the rocks and mud to the bank of the creek. The only building reasonably intact was Carl Bansemer's which had been pushed several feet off its foundation. Debris around the doors and windows blocked all exits.

Attracted to the Ennis home by cries for help, rescuers found that Sam Ennis had extricated himself and was trying to free his wife, Lucy, pinned by a beam. Lights were brought from the village and the rescuers dug into the cold mud and slime to release the imprisoned victims. Despite painful injuries, Lucy Ennis had already managed to save the life of her infant daughter, Gladys, who had been sleeping with them. The child had almost suffocated from having her mouth blocked by a clod of earth which Lucy was able to remove.

Shaken, but intact, Ennis helped rescue his three other children before faint cries attracted them to the back room of the house where James Warrington had been sleeping. As they freed him, Warrington warned that he could feel something soft beneath him. Digging carefully, the men located Mrs. Watkins who had been flung from her cottage next door. She was pulled from the rubble suffering from shock and countless rock splinters that made her skin look like a pincushion.

Mrs. Ennis had a broken collarbone, and Warrington a broken hip. Apart from assorted cuts and bruises, the children had miraculously escaped major injury.

In the darkness where the Watkins cottage had stood the two teenage children, Ruby and Thomas, pulled themselves from the rubble and looked around. There was no sign of their sister, Fernie. Then somewhere in the darkness a man began to call. Stumbling through the cloud of dust the youngsters fought through the jagged rocks to the voice but they no longer heard the man calling. Already water had backed up from the Oldman River which was dammed by the slide, but they managed to wade the waist-deep chill water and reach safety.

They did not know what had happened. Nor did they know where their mother or baby sister were and little suspected that their father and the rest of the night crew were trapped deep inside the ruined mine.

Lester Johnson had felt the wind lift their house a couple of feet off its foundation. Scarcely had it settled when there was a shuddering crash and the house toppled onto them. He heard his parents scream. He remembered nothing more until he revived to find himself lying between two enormous boulders which had crashed together over him, pinning him but sheltering him from the onslaught of falling rock. Through the haze of dust, he could see that day was breaking and that fires were burning a short distance away. He tried to crawl towards the light but a piece of lath that had been driven into his side caught on the rocks. He fainted.

When Lester regained consciousness, it was broad daylight and the dust had settled considerably. Through the opening between the rocks he could see Sam Ennis and others digging in the ruins of the Leitch home. He managed to break the lath and pull it from his side and crawl into the open. His night clothes had been torn from his body and he emerged from his rock womb like a new-born babe.

Nearly frozen, he managed to swim the creek and make his way to the Williams family who were so excited that no one noticed his nakedness or his wound. When Mrs. Williams examined him, she found feathers where the lath had driven through the mattress and penetrated his body. They bundled him into blankets and in an old iron wheelbarrow trundled him to Dr. Malcolmson's hospital. For the third time Lester passed out — this time from warmth and sleepiness.

Dr. Malcolmson's living-room had been converted into a hospital ward because the regular ward beside the house was already full. He plucked feathers from Lester as he would have from a chicken. Shortly after when Mrs. Watkins was brought in, the doctor switched from plucking feathers to prying out stone splinters.

In the ruins of the Leitch home, silence prevailed as George Bond and his fellow workers approached after freeing the Ennis family. By then day was breaking. Though the top had been sheered off the house and carried along with the crest of the slide, the remainder of the three-roomed house lay in a mess of collapsed walls. The rescue party found an opening in the rear and crawled into the back room. Here they found two girls, Jessie and Rose-Mary, pinned on the bed beneath a ceiling joist. They were unharmed and soon passed to safety. But the rescuers' relief at finding the girls alive soon turned to grief. In the next room beneath the mud and plaster they found the bodies of two of the four boys. In a third room, they unearthed the bodies of Alex Leitch and his wife. The remaining two boys, buried even deeper in the debris, were not found until the following day.

The Leitch's baby daughter had an astounding escape. She had been flung from the top floor of the demolished house and landed on a bale of hay that had been whisked from the destroyed livery stable a half mile away. Mrs. Bansemer, hearing the child's cry, directed searchers until the baby was found.

Fernie, the third of the Watkins children, also had a miraculous escape. She, too, had been tossed from her house and was lying cold and dirty behind some rocks when found by pit boss Edgar Ash.

As morning broke over the valley, the searchers began to appreciate for the first time the magnitude of the disaster. The evening before the sun had set on a peaceful scene, it rose now to reveal a river of rocks a mile and a half wide and over a mile long, fanning out from the base of the mountain. Above, where there had been a steep, heavily wooded slope, there was only a jagged slash on the mountain. Below the break rocks still

This massive boulder is part of the slide debris. Of over 100 people in the path of the slide, only twenty-three survived. Below are six of them, the Sam Ennis family. Standing with the crutch is Jim Warrington, one of the men trapped in the mine.

tumbled downward in clouds of grey limestone dust. The river which had coursed safely through its rocky banks was flooding rapidly, creating a lake and backing into Gold Creek.

As the searchers gazed with horror upon the sea of rock, they realized that there was no hope for the fifty or more men, women and children who had lived on the eastern flat beyond the row of cottages. Those not killed outright but trapped now faced certain drowning.

At the eastern edge of the slide, James Graham's log house was buried beneath a hundred feet of rock. Somewhere under the massive mound he lay with the bodies of his wife, sons, and the two Johnson boys. They found the old trapper, Andy Grissack, wrapped in his tent with an iron frying pan clutched in his hand. When the searchers rolled him over his scalp peeled like a layer of onion skin.

To the north of the farm of Alex Graham, dusty grey boulders, some still covered with the original shale and brush from the mountain top, lay deathlike and still. Neither his body, nor that of his wife, was ever found.

Behind the farm, the cemetery lay almost completely buried. To the west of the cemetery, rails of a section of the Frank and Grassy Mountain rail line were twisted grotesquely and ties slivered into fragments of wood. Along the CPR tracks, rock piled three times the height of a train marked where John McVeigh, Joe Britton, J.J. Scott and their twelve construction laborers lay buried.

Somewhere on the eastern flats under the mass of rocks George Williams, his wife and four children rested, as did his brother-in-law, Thomas Lock. The entire Vandusen family of four were gone, so were Mrs. William Warrington, her three children and their visitor, Alex Dixon. The cottage beside theirs containing the six Lancashire miners had vanished. The Ben Cunes family of four, together with ten or more unknown miners, lay covered by the death-dealing blanket of rocks.

A rumor persists that at least fifty men hoping to get work in the mine had arrived in Frank the evening before and pitched tents on the recreation field. While some old-timers insist that they were there and must have perished, other believe they had gone on to Blairmore. The truth lies beneath the rocks.

The body of Fred Farrington who had been eating his dinner on the mine tipple was found a quarter mile away on the western edge of the slide. No trace of his dinner companions, Tashigan and Clark, was ever found. The body of Thomas Delap, the newlywed engineer at the electric light plant, was not found for days and then only a short distance from the plant.

Where the livery stable had stood at the foot of the row of miners' cottages fate again had been inconsistent with bodies. Robert Watt who had been sleeping in the loft was never found. His assistant, Rochette, was located lying in rocks, looking almost as if asleep. Throughout the whole area, the bodies and broken limbs of horses were scattered in profusion.

The log cabin beside the stable was gone and with it the two Welsh miners. The body of the third occupant, Alfred Dawe, was found near the railway station. Astonishingly, his faithful fox terrier was uninjured and found wandering and whining near where the cabin had stood.

As dawn broke over the stricken town, a citizens' meeting was held and search parties organized. One group, which had been stumbling in the dangerous dark of the mountain side trying to locate the mine entrance, gazed with disbelief upon the sheered off surface. The slope above was a seething sea of stone, huge masses of rock still breaking away from the crumbling rim above. The mine bridge over which the locomotive had raced with inches to spare, lay twisted and broken in the icy, rising waters.

While the mine engineer sought to pinpoint the entrance with his transit, men spread over the rocks, collecting timber for a raft to cross the river. A rope was strung from bank to bank and the makeshift raft began to shuttle men and equipment to the wounded slope. Amidst still falling rocks they began their assault to free the trapped miners. Considering the damage to the mine entrance, however, it seemed impossible that any of the men inside would be alive. Nevertheless, the rescuers kept at their task, more from habit than hope. While some watched the slope above to warn of danger, others worked in shifts of fifteen minutes, tearing at the mess of rocks, shale and mine timbers.

In the meantime, word had been relayed through Cranbrook to Calgary and from there to eastern points. As was inevitable, the first reports were garbled and bordered on fantasy. Descriptions of the disaster ranged from a gigantic explosion in the mine to an earthquake, with over 100 bodies already found and upwards of 50 men imprisoned inside the mine.

The CPR acted promptly by sending a special train from Cranbrook to evacuate the stricken community. At the same time, the Dominion government dispatched William Pearce, Inspector of Mines, to take charge of the situation. While Inspector Davidson, NWMP officer in charge of the Pincher Creek sub-division, rode in with a sergeant and a constable to reinforce Constable Leard, a further force of ten police under Inspector Douglas was rushed from Calgary. They were joined by another contingent of twenty-five men from Macleod and Lethbridge. Their special train, loaded with correspondents from various newspapers, arrived at Frank at 4 a.m. April 30. The *Calgary Herald's* correspondent, impeccably attired, ensconced himself in a local hotel and began to send out reports without proper research. His were the source of much misinformation on the tragedy.

During the hectic day business establishments closed, partly from respect and partly because no one was interested in shopping. The hotel bars, by contrast, did a roaring business with those who had viewed the calamity and wished to forget as promptly as possible what they had seen.

In the little hospital and converted front room of Dr. Malcolmson's house, the doctor and his nurse, Miss Grassick, cared for the injured. They were pitifully few for only a handful of residents who had been touched by the sea of rocks lived to remember. Lester Johnson, bandaged to the armpits, reveled in the warmth. Jim Warrington, his hip re-set, struggled as he fought off the after effects of ether. Mrs. Watkins, knowing her children were safe, fretted over the absence of her husband. No one dared tell her that he was among the trapped men in the mine.

THE ENTOMBED MINERS

As Joe Chapman and his nineteen men trudged up the spur line to the mine entrance that morning of April 29, 1903, they had no premonition of danger. It was true that strange things had been happening in the mine. Two-foot timbers set one night had been found splintered by the day crew, and upraises where the coal had been removed silently closed overnight. But these occurrences had taken place four or five months before. Since then the belly of the Turtle had been quiet. There had been a minor earthquake the year the mine opened, but this tremor had had no apparent ill effect. Two young miners had been killed in a gas explosion the previous October but they apparently had been wearing the old style open flame lamps instead of the new safety lights.

The night crew left Tashigan at the mine tipple where he operated the scales and coal washing equipment. Then they entered the shaft via what had been a nearly vertical seam of coal about 30 feet above the river. The seam itself, varying in width from 9 to 30 feet, came from the direction of Goat Mountain, passed under the town of Frank and through Turtle Mountain in an almost north-south direction, paralleling the axis of the mountain itself. From the mouth of the mine, the drift rose sharply to a height of nearly 1,200 feet. Already the mine had been worked back some 5,000 feet. Because of the near vertical nature of the main vein, mining was a simple operation. The coal was merely worked loose and allowed to fall down the incline to the main manway where it was loaded on the mine cars and hauled by horse to the tipple on the outside.

At one time the mine had employed nearly 300 men, but in the winter of 1902 nearly one third had been laid off. The mine was now operating only one shift, with a night crew for timbering and maintenance purposes.

As the miners penetrated the tunnel, they dropped off to their duties. Alex Grant and his driver took one of the five horses stationed at the entrance and began checking the trackage. Fred Farrington and Alex Clark took other horses and started hauling out cars of coal left by the day shift. Timberman William Warrington set about his never-ending task of checking the mine timbers — testing, replacing damaged ones or setting up new ones.

As the night wore on, lamps glowed dimly in the tunnels and upraises. Some men worked alone, others in pairs. Towards 4 a.m. Clark and Farrington took loads of coal out to the mine tipple and sat down to eat their lunches with Tashigan.

Shortly afterward Grant and his driver felt a shock, like a severe bump. Thinking it was a gas explosion and fearing it might be followed by afterdamp (deadly carbon dioxide gas) they raced towards the mine entrance. The tunnel around them was heaving and twisting, sending down small showers of rock and coal. When they reached the end of it they found not daylight and safety but a mass of shattered timbers and fallen rock. As they gazed in horror they were joined by others running from the depths of the mine. One miner panicked at the sight of the blocked entrance and turned to flee. As he did so, he tripped and fell, wrenching his leg severely.

WHERE MINERS ESCAPE

X X SITE OF RESCUE DIG

The Frank slide and dammed Oldman River. Fortunately for the miners, their
tunnel emerged behind the boulder, protecting them from rocks still
hurtling down Turtle Mountain.
Charlie, one of the mine horses, amazingly survived several weeks in the black tunnel.
Unfortunately, the welcome of oats and brandy from his rescuers killed him.

Further back in the manway, Joe Chapman felt the earth's shudder. Then a blast of hot air picked him up and slammed him against the tunnel wall. He recovered and ran for almost a mile along the crazily heaving tracks to the entrance.

Dan McKenzie had been working in an upraise some way back when a sudden blast of air, followed by a shower of coal, flung him against the side of the mine and gashed his head. Realizing that something unusual had happened, he ignored the wound to his head and raced down the manway.

At the blocked entrance, breathless from their frantic dashes for safety, seventeen miners rested momentarily and then considered their position. One of them who had worked the mine from its opening day and who knew intimately every inch of the timbering and tracks examined the inside of their prison. He concluded that they were at least 300 feet from the outside. The news dismayed them, even though some of the more optimistic felt that they could not be more than 50 feet back. Leaving Warrington, whose leg had been severely squeezed in the heaving tunnel, the rest made their way to the lower level, hoping to find the exit there still intact. They were dismayed to discover that it was already filling with water from the dammed Oldman River. Even as they watched they saw the water rapidly backing up into the mine.

The mine was deathly quiet and the mountain had ceased to shudder as they made their way back to the entrance where Warrington and the other injured man waited. They now realized that their situation was grave. Cut off by rising water, sealed in by rock, they realized that if the air shafts had also been pinched their supply would soon be fouled. It was possible also that the upheaval had loosened pockets of gas that would collect in the upper regions of the tunnels.

Maintaining their calm, they returned bravely to their original work places and collected their tools. Back at the entrance they began to try to battle their way through the shattered timbers and crumbled rocks.

While they were working, McKenzie and two others climbed 300 feet up ladders to the Nicholson Level, as the old workings were called. Gas was already collecting. More disastrously, their investigations revealed that the air shafts had been completely sealed. They returned to their comrades with this discouraging news.

The men working at the entrance were making little or no progress against the snarled mass of timber and rocks. Panic began to rise. At that point one man took charge. Some say it was Joe Chapman, the foreman, others say it was Dan McKenzie, while others believe it was Charlie Farrell. Whichever man it was knew that a seam of coal outcropped on the mountain some distance from the main portal. Believing that they were close enough to the surface to break free through the outcrop, the man convinced the others to start digging. They did not know how far they were from the surface or whether they might encounter an insurmountable barrier of rock. What they did know, however, was that their air was becoming more foul, more and more unable to keep them alive.

In the cramped shaft the men had to work in relays of two or three — slowly but steadily swinging their picks. Towards mid-afternoon, three of them returned to the main entrance to examine once again the rubble. The impossibility of escape that way was obvious.

Under the increasing strain and diminishing oxygen supply, some of the men became excited, others morose. In the beginning they had sung to boost their courage, now they were quiet, hoping to conserve the fast faltering supply of air. Towards late afternoon they slumped exhausted against the mine wall. Only McKenzie and two others persevered.

Unexpectedly, McKenzie's pick drove into the open. A beam of brilliant sunlight blinded him and clean air bathed his face. The exhausted men, revived by the fresh air, renewed their fight for freedom. They quickly discovered that rocks still cascading down the mountainside prevented escaping via the new tunnel. Their morale now high, they started driving another shaft upwards through 36 feet of coal and clay. Thirteen hours after the slide had sealed them in, they broke into daylight behind boulders which shielded them from the rock falls.

McKenzie, the first man out, stared in astonishment. The slide fanned

The freed miners being escorted up Frank's main street with the slide in the background. After reaching safety, injured William Warrington in the wagon, learned that his wife, their three children and his friend were among the dead.

out from the base of Turtle Mountain like a giant's stubby-fingered hand of destruction on the valley floor. Small figures scrambled over the rocks, obviously searching. From a mass of broken timbers where the row of miners' cottages had stood, white smoke curled lazily into the late afternoon sky. Fifty yards below and to the left, a little knot of men battled the rubble blocking the mine entrance.

McKenzie called. They looked up, whooping with joy as they saw him. There was a scrambled rush across the treacherous slope, a grasping of hands and exchange of news.

For John Watkins whose anguished glance had revealed only a sea of rocks and mud where his home should have been, the news was good. His three children had escaped and his wife was recovering in hospital.

For William Warrington who had to be lifted on a plank because of his injured leg, there was tragic news. Only rock marked his temporary dwelling among the jackpine. Even the possibility of a minor miracle was erased when he looked at the downcast faces of his rescuers. For him there

was only the realization that his wife, three children and friend, Alex Dixon, lay buried beneath the massive limestone grave.

The seventeen men were hurried down the mountain and across the makeshift ferry. Since Farrington, Clark and Tashigan were not among them, the tabulators added their names to the growing casualty list. A waiting wagon carried Warrington up the main street and across the flat to Dr. Malcolmson's hospital. While the other miners sought relatives and friends, some stopped at the hotel bar to wet throats still dry from fear.

Miracles are seldom wrought by one person. The escape of the miners entombed in Turtle Mountain was no exception. An ingenious and daring suggestion by one man pointed the way; the courage and strength of all seventeen to follow that suggestion saved their lives.

AMONG THE DEAD

All that day of April 29 massive rocks shook loose from the scarred crest and bounded down the sheer slope. Suddenly conscious that another enormous slice overhung the untouched part of the village, people fled their cottages, piling household goods into wagons or wheelbarrows. Whole families vacated the town and were loaded onto the special CPR train for transportation to Blairmore and points west.

A citizens' meeting had been convened by the president of the Board of Trade early in the morning. Search parties were sent into the ruins but by nightfall only twelve bodies were recovered and removed to the temporary morgue in the schoolhouse. Most were so badly mutilated that identification had to be made through clothing or documents, or from the location where they were found.

For some it was a day of wonderment and awe. Ellen Thornley was horrified to realize that except for a whim she and her brother would have been sleeping in the shoe shop that now lay beneath the rocks. Les Ferguson, who had parted company with Robert Watt a few hours before, searched unsuccessfully for his friend's body. Jack Leonard, returning from Pincher Creek after a successful hay-buying trip, gazed in disbelief on the rubble where his camp had been. He alone of the entire McVeigh and Poupore crew was alive.

There were the two Welsh miners and Alfred Dawe who should have been on the CPR train, safely heading eastward and home — except for the mistake in their reservations. Dawes' terrier survived, they didn't. Charles and Robert Chestnut also survived. The only reason, however, was that the cabin they were impatiently waiting to move into was occupied by the three delayed men.

The first hero of the tragedy was Sid Choquette who had scrambled through the wilderness of rock to warn the approaching *Spokane Flyer*. An early rumor circulated that he had gone insane as a result of the awful scenes he had seen, but it was not so. Another reported that grateful passengers of the train presented him with a gold watch and the CPR guaranteed him a job for life. Again the rumors were untrue. Choquette and Conductor Pettit were given cheques for $25 and letters of commendation. Later, Sid transferred to the Illinois Central Railroad and remained until his retirement in the 1930s.

Early on the morning of April 30, the special train arrived from Macleod, carrying twenty-five officers and men of the NWMP under the command of Inspector Primrose. Doctors Kennedy and Edwards of Macleod accompanied the train with their nurses, but there was little they could do. The need for doctors and nurses was not acute since most of those overtaken by the flood of limestone had been killed instantly and the survivors had already received medical attention from Dr. Malcolmson and Nurse Grassick. Kennedy and Edwards returned almost at once to their own practices.

The following day, Premier Haultain arrived. He immediately held a meeting with the Board of Trade. As a result, a party of engineers and mountain experts were dispatched to the top of Turtle Mountain to determine what danger might remain.

In the meantime, 128 men from the camp at Breckenridge and Lund who had been scheduled to begin work on the Frank and Grassy Mountain Railroad were brought from Fernie and put to work clearing the river to prevent further serious flooding. Others were organized into crews to build a road around the north end of the slide.

As rock had ceased falling by the morning of May 1, many townspeople began returning to their homes. Plans were laid by J.S. McCarthy, acting mine superintendent, to re-open the mine and explore the full extent of the damage. One of the employees succeeded in entering the mine through the tunnel excavated by the trapped miners and reported that the main tunnel was not severely damaged. He estimated damage at about $75,000.

When the exploratory party returned from the summit of Turtle Mountain, their report was both reassuring and disturbing. Along the section overlooking Frank they had found huge fissures, some over 150 feet deep, but had not detected evidence of another potential slide. As a result Premier Haultain, after assuring himself that there was no destitution among the survivors, began the slow, two-hour climb over the slide to his special train.

At the east edge of the rocks he was met by A. McHenry, the CPR's Chief Engineer who had spent the day watching the mountain top through binoculars. He was convinced that it was shifting towards the edge. Any moment he expected more gigantic slices to plunge down on the remainder of the town.

At this news, Haultain and his party at once returned and held a second meeting with the Board of Trade and Inspector Primrose. They decided to evacuate Frank immediately. The injured were put aboard special cars and transported half a mile east to the NWMP barracks which became a temporary hospital. By nightfall Frank was deserted, displaced citizens waiting with dread for news that a new fall had obliterated their homes and businesses.

A "dead-line" was drawn at Frank's west end and patrolled night and day by the police. No one was permitted to enter the area at night and during the day only those having legitimate business were allowed through. Inside Frank, the police maintained a rigid patrol. As a result, not a single case of looting occurred while the town was empty.

One of the few people permitted through the police cordon was Harry J. Matheson, editor of the *Frank Sentinel*. Matheson, displaying true journalistic spirit, rolled his press despite the potential peril of another slide. He wrote:

"The conduct of our citizens when the disaster occurred here on Wednesday, was praiseworthy in the extreme . . . ." But he also noted: "The arrival of the police was very timely as already vicious and cowardly elements, of which there are some in every community, had early taken to the bottle and drunken rowdies were strongly in evidence on our streets."

The edition appeared on time.

To Matheson fell the unhappy task of setting in print the list of casualties — many of whom he had known. He listed seventy-six, but no one will ever know how many really died in the battering wind, pulverizing rocks, suffocating dust, or rising water. No one knows for certain how many men were in the construction camp that night, since all records were buried; no one knows how many, like Robert Watt, had crossed the fateful dividing line of Gold Creek to visit or sleep in the temporary shacks and tents in the eastern flats. Rumor persists that about fifty men were camped on the recreation ground, now buried under rock and mud. While many of the casualties were listed as dead because of their continued absence, the bulk of evidence was circumstantial. Only twelve bodies were recovered.

While in later years many persons claimed to be survivors because they had been resident in Frank at the time, technically only those who had been "in the rocks" were true claimants to the honor. Others, like Lillian Clark, Jack Leonard or Ellen and John Thornley were survivors only in the sense that fate had dictated their presence elsewhere.

The real survivors were few: Mrs. John Watkins and her three children; Sam and Lucy Ennis and their four children; James Warrington; Lester Johnson; the three Leitch girls; and Annie Bansemer with her seven children. In all, twenty-three fortunate people.

To these must be added the seventeen miners, but the inadequacy of records has drawn a curtain over some of them. Those known include Joseph Chapman, Dan McKenzie, Evan Jones, Wm. Warrington, Alex W. Grant, "Shorty" Dawson, Alex McPhail, John Watkins, Charles Farrell and Charles Elick. There were seven others whose courage had enabled them to survive.

THE AFTERMATH

For nine days a careful watch was kept on the shoulder of Turtle Mountain directly above Frank. On May 10, Premier Haultain returned for a meeting with CPR engineer McHenry. After an encouraging report that there seemed to be no movement, Haultain advised the residents they were free to return to their homes.

Despite this reassuring news, there was no stampede back to Frank. Merchants and hotel keepers re-opened their businesses, but ten days later only two houses had been re-occupied. Since the mine was still closed, however, there was no great incentive for people to leave the assured safety of Blairmore. Even the hotels had few guests.

Dominion Avenue in 1910 with Turtle Mountain and the massive scar from the slide. Because of the threat of another slide, the Dominion government ordered the community to be moved to a safer location.

On Sunday, May 24, a large group of sightseers flocked from surrounding towns to view the damage. Their curiosity was interrupted when 100 pounds of dynamite being thawed by the railway builders exploded. A panicky crowd raced for shelter. Fortunately, no one was injured.

On May 30, workers at the mine reported they had made an opening to the old workings. As they explored the manways they found, to their amazement, Charlie, one of the mine horses. He had survived both the cave-ins and days of starvation. The others horses, stabled near the mine entrance, had all been killed. Charlie had survived by drinking seepage water and gnawing wood from the coal cars and timbers. He was unable to survive the welcome of his rescuers, however, for shortly after he succumbed to an overdose of brandy and oats.

When the explorations revealed that the main workings were intact for some 5,000 feet, Samuel Gebo, one of the partners in the mine, announced that it would be re-opened immediately. But hard luck now started to prevail. In 1905 two serious fires drove the miners out, while seepage from the lake which had been formed by the rock slide made operations very difficult. To avoid this seepage a new shaft-type mine was started some distance back from the original workings.

In 1908, H.L. Frank died. For months he had been confined to a private sanatorium, his mind broken by memories of his ill-fated mining venture. Subsequently, the mine was sold.

Following the slide the Dominion government sent R.G. McConnell and R.W. Brock of the Geological Survey of Canada to investigate. By early June 1903 their report was completed and noted, in part:

"The management state that the mine was in first class condition before the catastrophe, that the walls were solid, that there were no more movements or breaking away of the hanging wall than is usual in coal mines, and that the timbers were not under undue strain. Mr. Chestnut, a miner, states that slight movements were noticeable during the last seven months. These were particularly liable to occur between one and three in the morning. He describes them as like the starting and shuddering of a ship struck by a wave. Mr. Chapman (the foreman) also stated that these shocks were most frequent between the hours of one and three in the morning. These tremors were somewhat alarming to the miners, and some are said to have left the mine on account of them.

"It is also reported that lately the coal has been mined with unusual ease, often running itself, so that the miners were taken off contract work and put upon day work. Rock from the hanging wall is said to have been falling in and mixing with the coal, so that men had to be employed in picking it out when the cars were dumped.

"Cyrus Morris, formerly underground superintendent, stated that for the last seven months, there had been a general squeeze in the ground between 3,500 and 5,000 feet in the tunnel. The coal could be kept up only with difficulty. It was broken and would mine itself."

On the final reason for the slide, the report stated:

"The snapping of the last threads supporting the peak which broke away, that is the final cause of the slide, was in all probability due to the temperature conditions during and preceding the morning of April 29.

"The night of the slide was excessively cold. The miners say that it was colder than any night during the winter. Those outside state that the temperature was down to zero. The day before and the preceding days had been very hot, so that the fissures in the mountain must have been filled with water, on which the frost would act with powerful effect.

"The rock slide cannot, therefore, be considered as due to a single cause, but rather, like so many phenomena in nature, to a combination of causes, cumulative in their effects. The chief of these were the structure and condition of the mountain, aided by exceptional atmospheric and other natural conditions, and also, possibly, by slight readjustments in the lower strata attendant on mining operations."

Frank's problems did not end when the massive slide stabilized for the community still lived under the shadow of death. As the report noted:

"The fractured zone surrounding the old break is bound sooner or later to fall away, but whether it falls gradually in small comparatively harmless blocks, or in large destructive masses depends upon future conditions, which cannot be foretold. The shattered mass between the north and south peaks does not menace the town, as the falling material will travel over the former slide. Moreover, the fracturing is so complete, that it is rapidly falling in individual blocks, which, though large, are yet not large enough for their momentum to carry them to the base of the mountain . . . .

"That part of the north peak lying east of the fissure, 150 feet from the face, along which it slipped during our observations, threatens the mouth of the main tunnel of the mine, since, if it falls in one block, it will certainly reach the base of the mountain near the edge of the former slide. More danger to the town is apprehended from the fissures that exist behind and further to the west of the north peak. These fissures are narrow, but are wide enough to admit water, and the pressure of the rock above may keep them closed until the undermining action of the water, or some other cause, liberates the superincumbent mass and a slide results. The safety of the town depends upon the stability of the shoulder protruding eastward from the north peak . . . . The breaking away of the central portion of the mountain, which is going on continuously, is also tending to weaken this northern shoulder. If the town is to remain inhabited in its present position, these northern fissures must be closely watched. They are not likely to slip or extend suddenly (although, as stated above, there is always some liability of their doing so), and for this reason the upper portion of the town is not considered to be in any great immediate danger. If, however, any signs of slipping along the fissures some distance back from the north peak are detected, the town ought to at once be evacuated.

"The town of Frank might exist on its present site uninjured for ages, but there will always be a possibility of a second destructive slide. The fact that the north shoulder withstood the shock of the first slide and was so solid that a snow cornice over its face was not broken down, is no proof that it is too solid to fall. A succession of seasons with unusually heavy precipitations and rapid changes of temperature, a slight earthquake shock, which is by no means an impossibility, or the closing of the chambers in the mine after the coal has been drawn, perhaps long after the inhabitants have lost all dread of the mountain, may snap the supports which retain this mass in place and start it on a career of destruction.

"Since this possibility must always overhang the town it certainly seems in the interests of safety that it be moved a short distance up the valley, beyond the reach of danger."

Additional examinations during forthcoming years reinforced the conclusions of the original report, especially since several large fissures opened in the section overlooking Frank. In 1911 the Dominion government appointed a Commission of two geologists and an engineer to investigate further and recommend a policy. The Commission noted that the cracks in the rocks near the summit were widening and also agreed that another slide could happen. While they felt that the mining company could not be blamed for the first slide, they could be held responsible if a second occurred. They recommended that Frank be moved to a safer location north of the CPR tracks. As a consequence, the Dominion government ordered the move.

While the shift in location had a disruptive effect, it did not cause the death of the once flourishing community. The coal mine was responsible. It closed in 1917, not because company officials feared that it might cause

Frank in 1910 from the balcony of the Union Bank looking north toward the buildings of the new Frank.

a second rock fall but because it was no longer competitive. What remained of Frank was torn down, moved, or fell into decay.

By then the old stagecoach road through the north end of the slide had been replaced by another which traversed the slide at the base of Turtle Mountain. A twisting route through the boulders, it is still used, emerging at the east end near an abandoned lime kiln. Not far from the kiln, somewhere under the rocks, lies James Graham's ranch house and its six occupants. The western end is close to where the row of miners' houses stood that tragic night of April 29, 1903.

In 1922, while widening the west end, workmen uncovered skeletons and parts of a cradle. Old-timers believed they were the remains of the Clark family. The bones and other grim mementoes were buried where they were found, a memorial now identifying the location. In 1949, while a steam shovel was loading CPR trains with ballast rock, some of the original trackage and a case of footwear that might have come from Thornley's shoe store was uncovered. In 1932 a new highway was built north of the railway line, a route which today is part of Highway Number 3 linking southern Alberta and B.C. through the Crowsnest Pass.

Over the years, grim reminders of the devastation from that epic 100 seconds have gradually disappeared. Included were the wheels of the coal car which Choquette and his companions were spotting as the slide began. No one bothered to preserve them and they were melted in a reduction furnace.

One thing that has not disappeared, however, are myths that arose even before the last unstable rocks crashed downward. The tragedy of the slide itself, its sixty or more bodies still entombed; the self-rescue of the trapped miners; and the narrow escapes of many residents is dramatic enough without any elaboration. Nevertheless, there were those who tried to change the truth or capitalize on it.

For instance, despite the fact that twenty-three people came out of the rocks and another seventeen from the mine, and despite the fact that nine-tenths of the town's population was unscathed, unscrupulous persons were able to pass themselves off during the summers of 1903 and 1904 in the eastern United States as the "sole survivor." The Union Bank stood for eight more years on its original foundations but hardly had it been torn down in 1911 than a rumor started that it had been buried, together with $500,000 in American silver dollars.

The miraculous escape of baby Marion Leitch who was flung from her shattered home onto a bale of hay has also been distorted many times. Romanticists and pseudo-historians created the myth of "Frankie Slide" and had her found everywhere from on a rock to dead in her mother's arms. She was also credited with being the only survivor, although her two sisters and a score of other citizens also survived. When Marion Leitch grew up she married Lawrence McPhail and lived until 1977.

Today, the cascade of death which ruptured from Turtle Mountain still lies like an enormous scar across the valley of the Crowsnest Pass. To tens of thousands of motorists who pause at the viewpoint each year, it is a reminder of 100 seconds of wind, rock and dust — an awesome tombstone where lie at least seventy-six people.

HILLCREST MINE DISASTER

BREAK OF DAWN

The sun peeked over the horizon, glanced at the scarred face of Turtle Mountain, scanned the crags and peaks of the Livingstone Range and then, as if satisfied, leaped hot and red into the June morning sky. It sent its rays glimmering over the mining communities of Burmis, Leitch Collieries, Maple Leaf and Bellevue, into the peaceful flats between Bellevue and Hillcrest, over the ghostly ruins of the Frank Slide, and on through the gap between Goat and Turtle Mountains. It lit the tipple of Hillcrest Collieries, then followed the mine tracks round the gently sweeping mountainside until it found the concrete mine buildings nestling in the valley between Hillcrest and Turtle Mountains. Here it caught the eyes of William Adkin, fireboss, as he stepped from the mouth of Mine No. 1, forcing him to squint against the brilliance of the new day dawning in the Crowsnest Pass.

It was 6:20 a.m., June 19, 1914. Adkin had just completed an inspection of the mine in preparation for the morning shift due to arrive at 7 a.m. As part of his responsibility, he posted a notice on the bulletin board in the lamphouse. It advised that he had found pockets of gas in certain sections of the mine, some cave-ins and rock fall in other parts. That done, he checked with timekeeper Robert Hood and went off duty.

The Hillcrest mine was considered the safest and best-run operation in the Crowsnest Pass. It had been discovered in 1900 by Charles Plummer Hill, a United States customs officer who spent his free time scouring the mountains for minerals. Hill had been in no hurry to develop the property and it was January 1905 before serious mining started.

In 1909 Hill sold the mines, originally known as the Hillcrest Coal and Coke Company, to a group of Montreal developers. They reorganized the project under the name of Hillcrest Collieries Limited and invested

A rescue team hurries into Hillcrest Mine. On the hillside residents wait anxiously for news of over 200 trapped sons, fathers and husbands.

large sums of money to enlarge and modernize the operation.

Hill's original Mine No. 1 entered the mountain through a rock tunnel some 200 feet long, then dipped down Slant No. 1 for another 1,200 feet. From here radiated an intricate series of tunnels and passageways. Later, a second mine was opened about 500 feet to the south and it was known as Mine No. 2. By June 1914 this mine descended gently into the side of the mountain, along Slant No. 2 to a distance of 2,400 feet. These workings were joined to Slant No. 1 by two main intersecting tunnels, Level 1 and Level 2 South. Again, a complicated pattern of shafts and sloping runways ran from them to give access to the coal seams.

The third major section of the mine was opened in 1912. Known as Level 1 North, it swept in a huge semi-circle from a point 900 feet down Slant No. 2. Unlike the other two major workings, there was only one entrance to this part of the mine.

By June 1914, Hillcrest Collieries had 377 men on the payroll. Most of them lived in Hillcrest, although some came from the neighboring village of Bellevue and from houses and cottages scattered along the valley floor. The majority were married, earning an average of $125 a month, and despite periodic layoffs, enjoying a high standard of living.

Because of over-production, the mine was closed June 17-18 and scheduled to re-open on June 19. Accordingly, on the 18th, a pit committee of Frank Pearsons, president of the Miner's Union, with miners George Pounder and James Gurtson, toured the three major workings. They found them in satisfactory condition for resumption of work on Friday morning, June 19.

Fireboss Daniel Briscoe — one of whose duties was to inspect the mine for accumulations of coal dust, gas, or any other dangerous condition — went on duty at 3 p.m. Briscoe found gas in several sections of the mine and posted warning signs, but he reported that the ventilation was good and that there was plenty of moisture. Because of the highly explosive nature of coal dust, a vital safety factor was adequate moisture to dampen the dust and reduce the danger of explosion. At 11 o'clock that evening, he was relieved by fireboss William Adkin who, during his night shift, checked on the presence of gas, coal dust and moisture, then remained until the morning shift came on duty at 7 a.m.

One man who missed the morning shift was William Dodd, sixty-three, the oldest miner employed by Hillcrest Collieries. An old-timer in the Pass, he worked in almost every mine from Lethbridge to Fernie in British Columbia. Old Bill was damned if he was going to start work on a Friday. He stayed home — a decision that probably saved his life.

Dan Cullinen was employed on the afternoon shift. But when his friend, J.D. "Knicky Knack" Redmonson, developed a pain in his side, Cullinen took his place on the morning crew. As a consequence, Redmonson would live; his friend, die.

Tom Corkill, who had already survived a terrible blast in the Kenmore mines, went to work that morning with a feeling of nostalgia. This was his last shift in the Hillcrest workings. He had bought a homestead in the Lethbridge area and would be leaving for it next day.

Thomas Dugdale of Bellevue awoke at 6 a.m. to hear three of his brothers stirring in the house. The oldest of five Dugdale boys, Tom had arrived in Canada from Scotland and found work in the Bellevue mines. Shortly after he started, an explosion snuffed out the lives of thirty of his fellow miners. Tom had been off duty that day.

Following the death of their father, Tom's brothers — John, Robert, Andrew and Peter, with their mother — joined him in Canada. All five brothers eventually started working for Hillcrest Collieries. Today, Robert, Andrew and John, who was the assistant timekeeper on the morning shift, were preparing for work. Thomas, glad that he and Peter were on the afternoon shift, went back to sleep.

Meanwhile the buckers, the timber packers, the bratticemen and others who worked the underground tunnels left their homes to rendezvous at the mine tipple and climb the road leading to the mine buildings. One who did not climb was Steve Belopotosky, a regular on the early shift. As a favor to a friend whose wife was arriving from Britain that afternoon, he, too, had traded shifts.

Rod Wallis and his brother-in-law, William Neath, walked mechanically up the road. Tired of mining, they looked forward to Monday when they would be headed for their homes in Nova Scotia where they intended to resume farming. Fate had decreed, however, that neither would ever again see their home province.

By 6:45 a.m. the roadway was alive with some 250 men climbing towards a rendezvous with fate. About halfway up they lost sight of Hillcrest as the road entered the little valley that nestled between Hillcrest and Turtle mountains.

Turtle Mountain had special significance for one man who climbed that morning. Charles Elick had been one of twenty men on night duty at the Frank mine on the morning of April 29, 1903, when 90 million tons of rock broke from the face of Turtle Mountain and swept down the slope. Three miners had been killed at the mine tipple while Elick and sixteen

Hillcrest in 1914 with rubble from the Frank slide at upper left.

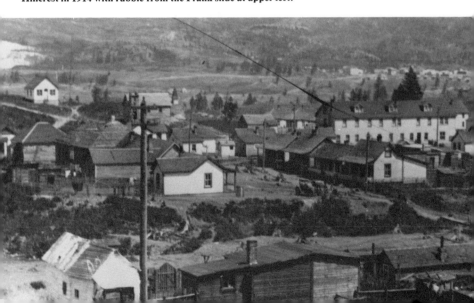

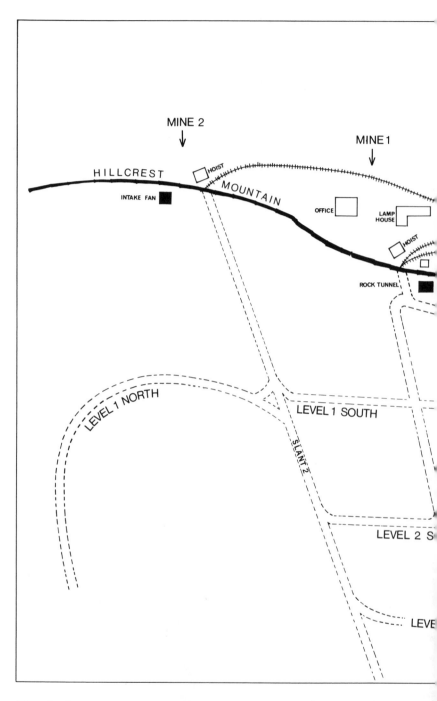

While the above map was copied from the original blueprint, only the main passageways are indicated. In reality, intricate patterns of tunnels and slopes interlaced the whole

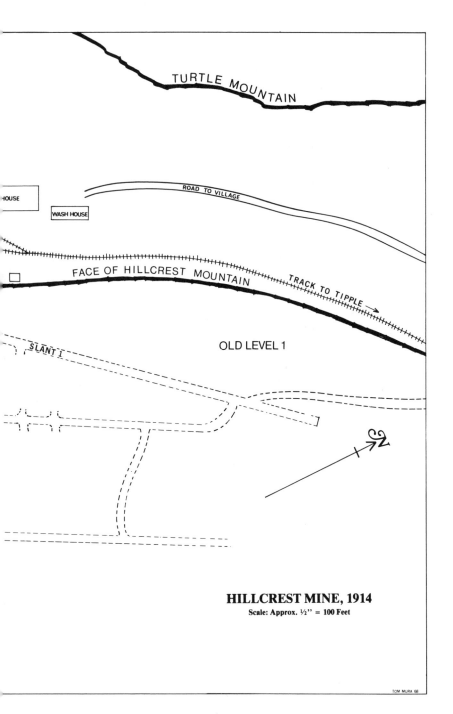

TURTLE MOUNTAIN

ROAD TO VILLAGE

HOUSE

WASH HOUSE

FACE OF HILLCREST MOUNTAIN

TRACK TO TIPPLE →

OLD LEVEL 1

SLANT I

HILLCREST MINE, 1914

Scale: Approx. ½" = 100 Feet

TOM MURA 68

area from Slant No. 2 northward and on both sides of Level 1 North. Evidence points to tunnel 33 near the center of the drawing as the point of explosion.

Miners ready to go underground at Hillcrest in 1912.

companions were trapped inside the mine. With the mine entrance blocked off, the ventilation shafts destroyed and deadly gas filtering through the workings, Elick and his mates had fought panic and exhaustion and dug for thirteen hours through a narrow seam of coal to the surface. This day Charles Elick was not to be so fortunate.

The Hillcrest Collieries buildings were on two levels. The roadway ended on a lower level, which contained the concrete washhouse and the engine room. Twenty feet above this level was the mine yard which contained a machine repair shop, a small shelter for horses, a combined office and supply building and the lamphouse. The entrances to both mines were on this level with a hoist house at the mouth of each mine. The mine railroad, along which coal cars were hauled to the tipple around the corner of the mountain, used this level as a roadbed.

As the men reached the lower level, those who worked outside the mines broke ranks and went to their places of work, while 228 men filed into the lamphouse. Here they picked up their equipment, their lamps and two brass tags with each man's number stamped upon them. From the lamphouse they crossed to the timekeeper's office where they checked in with Robert Hood, the methodical timekeeper who had the reputation of never having cheated a miner, or let one slip an unworked hour past him.

The majority of the men who tramped through the timekeeper's office at 7 a.m. were in their late twenties or early thirties, most related by

blood or marriage. The oldest was Robert Muir, fifty-four; the youngest, Alex Petrie, seventeen. Alex and his two brothers, James and Robert, lived with their widowed mother in Hillcrest where she operated a cafe with her two daughters.

One of them, John B. McKinnon, was known as the "Samson of the Pass." He stood 6 ft. 4 inches, weight 215 pounds and was reputed to be the strongest miner in Western Canada. A week previously at Frank he had picked up a 480-pound piece of railway track and hoisted it over his head for the amusement of his friends.

As they passed through the timekeeper's office, each man left one brass identification check with Robert Hood and kept the second. This way any man still in the mine could be identified if the second brass tag was missing. Because fireboss William Adkin had reported gas in several tunnels, Mine Superintendent James S. Quigley entered first. With him was a team of bratticemen — specialists whose job was to maintain the system of screens which controlled the flow of air through the mines.

Air for the shafts was drawn in by a huge steam-driven fan and forced into Level 1 North. Inside the mine, the direction of flow was controlled by a series of brattices, or screens, to ventilate those areas where men were working or in which undue amounts of gas had collected. From Level 1 North, the air flowed northward in controlled streams and was drawn out by a second giant fan near the entrance to Mine No. 1. Since the miners carried no oxygen, their survival depended upon the smooth functioning of these two fans. When gas was reported at any sector, the bratticemen re-directed the air flow to channel any accumulated gas back into the main air stream and exhaust it from the area.

Quigley and his men were followed within fifteen minutes by the rest of the miners. Most entered through the rock tunnel and dispersed to their various places by descending Slant No. 1. About fifty men entered the second mine, the bulk of them proceeding into the North 1 Level.

Before entering the mine, Sam Charlton, the fireboss who relieved Adkin, stopped at the powder house to pick up a supply of blasting powder and material from John Dugdale, popularly known as "Jock, the powder monkey." After signing for the powder, Charlton went into Mine No. 1. As he worked towards old Level 1, he set off several charges.

In other parts of the mine, men moved through the inky blackness, paths illuminated only by their Wolf Safety Lamps. Like ants in a giant anthill, they moved surely and expertly to their jobs, each knowing that in many instances his life and others depended on the quality of his workmanship. Some repaired and checked the mine tracks, some laid new rails, some installed new supporting timbers. Bratticemen constantly checked the flow of air, mechanics and electricians moved from electric engines to pumps and carpenters hammered away in the tomb-like darkness. Miners dug the coal then buckers shoved it along the slopes and chutes to the main passageways. Here it was loaded into mine cars and hauled by horses along the Levels to main Slants. The mine cars were then hooked onto a continuous cable system and drawn to the surface by the hoists just outside the mine entrances.

At these entrances, young men known as "rope-riders" unhooked the cars and shunted them onto the tracks outside. That morning Charles Ironmonger was the rope-rider at Mine 1, while Fred Kurigatz performed the same function at the other mine.

At 8 a.m. fireboss John Ironmonger checked in at the timekeeper's office. He picked up a supply of blasting powder from Jock, then stopped for a brief chat with his son, Charles, before going down into Level 1 North. Another of his sons, Sam, was on duty as a timber racker boss. After checking the dust content, moisture level and air circulation, Ironmonger set off five charges to blast more coal face open for the miners.

At 9 a.m. eight more miners passed through the lamphouse, collected their lamps and brass checks and went into the timekeeper's office. Hood passed six of them, but refused to let two into the mine when he detected the smell of liquor. Although Hood weighed only 140 pounds, there was no argument from the miners. They left the brass checks on his counter and returned their equipment to the lamphouse. That done, they wended their way back to the Miner's Hall to supplement their liquid intake. Without thinking, Hood picked up the two checks and hung them on the board with the others.

Down in the village, eight-year-old Jonathan Penn heard the school bell and raced out of the house. Without a glance towards the mine where his father and older brother worked, he ran across the flats and got into his desk by the window in time to escape the teacher's questioning eye.

At the Petrie Cafe, two men lingered over cups of coffee before walking over to the Miner's Hall for some stiffer refreshment. Charles

Elick's wife, expecting their child, began her daily round of house chores. Three men at the Miner's Hall, who should have been at work, contemplated the amber fluid in their glasses and philosophically pondered the meaning of wet circles on the table top. At the same time James Quigley's wife was walking two younger children to their new house completed the week before.

Alex May, outside engineer whose duty it was to inspect and maintain the two giant fans which blew in and exhausted the air in the workings, finished his inspection of the intake fan and crossed over to inspect the second.

Deep in Old Level 1, fireboss Sam Charlton, married barely a month, prepared two charges of powder in a coal face at tunnel 32. Normally, he would have uncoiled the firing cable which he carried wound around his leg, taken the battery from his pocket, connected them and set off the explosion with a firing key. For some reason, he hesitated.

Thomas Bardsley, a miner in Level 1, South, raised his pick to a slab of coal. The pick never fell.

HOLOCAUST

In that instant, somewhere in the miles of narrow, dark tunnels, a lamp flared, or a spark flew, or an electric cable shorted. The ever-present gas that hugged the tunnel roofs caught fire, skipped with lightning speed to a pocket of coal dust. In a fraction of a second, there was a massive explosion that triggered a second — and possibly a third — earth-shuddering blast.

Thomas Bardsley was transfixed in death by the violence of the explosion that cracked through the passages. His pick still clutched in upraised hands, his shirt collar blown 40 feet away, he stared with lifeless eyes at a seam of coal.

Alex May, working at the mouth of Mine No. 1, was dropped to his knees by the blast. When he looked back at the fan he had just inspected, he saw an ominous brown cloud of smoke rising from the ventilation shaft. The fan was motionless.

General Manager John Brown, who had just seen the roof of a hoist house crumple from the impact of an invisible fist, ran towards the mine entrance. Jock Dugdale raced out of his powder room: "Mr. Brown, there's a fire in the mine!"

"My God! It's worse than that," Brown replied. "Get an electrician, quick."

As Dugdale raced for an electrician, outside workers converged on the mine entrance.

In the village school, Jonathan Penn lost track of what the teacher was saying. He watched instead a plume of brown smoke climb slowly into the morning sky. Then he saw that people were flooding from their houses and running towards the mine. There was no more school that day.

The first man found by the outside workers was Charles Ironmonger, the rope-rider at Mine No. 1. The explosion which raced up the main tunnels from deep in the mine had picked him up and hurled him 60 feet against the hoist house, at the same time blowing down the 8-inch thick concrete wall. Although Ironmonger was still alive, he was scarcely breathing. They placed him on a wagon and rushed him to the little village hospital, but he died a few moments later. He was the first known casualty.

Others, heedless of the danger of another blast, raced to No. 1, only to find that the blast had jammed the mouth with fallen rock, wrecked mine cars and smashed timbers. There was no way in — or out — of the rock tunnel.

At the entrance to Mine No. 2, the destruction was repeated. The other rope-rider, Fred Kurigatz, was killed instantly after being thrown against the hoist house. Here the blast had lifted the roof from the building and caved in the concrete wall facing the mine. By some miracle, the hoist engine was still operable and the cable undamaged.

Two men rushed into the mouth of No. 2 but were driven out by gas and smoke, one of them barely making it to safety. Another, searching for his brother, rushed in and out several times but was driven back. He had to abandon his search.

Meanwhile, the electrician had managed to restart the fan above Mine No. 1 and reverse the wiring so that it began to draw air from the mines. Since the fan at Mine No. 2 was still functioning, it meant that both fans were sucking gas laden air from the corridors. Brown's quick action saved many lives among the miners who had survived the explosion but were now trapped in the gas-filled mine.

The explosions — one survivor reported hearing three separate blasts

Charles Ironmonger, junior, and Sam Ironmonger were among the 189 victims. Most had died from the explosion or blackdamp before rescuers, opposite page, could reach them.

which seemed to come so close together that they were one — had burned the oxygen out of the air. Left now was deadly carbon dioxide, called "blackdamp" or "afterdamp" by the miners. Air containing only 13 per cent carbon dioxide is sufficient to cause unconsciousness and death after prolonged exposure. Following the gigantic explosion it was estimated that nearly 50 per cent of the remaining air was composed of carbon dioxide.

The time of the explosions was placed at 9:30 a.m. A few minutes later three men — George Wild, Arthur Crowther and Antonio Stella — staggered from the mouth of Mine No. 2. They had been working only a short distance inside the entrance and had miraculously escaped the deadly blast that swept up Slant No. 2.

By then a call for help had been sent to Blairmore, where a government rescue car with full equipment was stationed. In the meantime the few men left on the surface worked frantically to clear the wreckage around the entrance to Mine No. 2. As there was no hope of clearing Mine No. 1, they concentrated on putting the second hoist into operation. With each passing minute, more and more white-faced men arrived from the village.

At Burmis Mines, about 2½ miles from Hillcrest, word of the disaster quickly reached the Royal North-West Mounted Police, and Corporals Frederick John Mead and Arthur Grant, with Constable William Hancock, raced to the scene on horseback.

The police arrived to find women and children swarming around the mine. "People were frantically trying to push through to see if their loved

ones were anywhere in sight," said Constable Hancock later. "Having heard the explosion, and knowing their men had already gone to work, and would be in the mine, they were still hopeful that some miracle may have spared them."

Fifteen minutes after the appearance of the first three survivors a second group of men staggered from the smoke-shrouded entrance. Malcolm Link and Charles Jones had been working together in Level 1 North a short distance beyond Wild, Crowther and Stella. Jones was knocked flat by the force of the explosion, but managed to crawl along the tracks. "I was lucky to get out," he said later. "We men on the North Level were not very far from the entrance and to that those of us who were rescued owe our lives."

Jack Maddison and John Moorehouse, who were nearly 1,500 feet from the entrance, were knocked from the bench on which they were kneeling. "I heard a loud report," said Maddison, "and realized that something had happened. I made a rush for the chute and up the slope. It was a long walk and I felt very keenly the effect of the gas. At times I felt inclined to lie down but I did not yield to the inclination."

On his way to the surface, he was joined by John Toth, who stumbled from a side tunnel. Together they picked their way through fallen rock and timber, wrecked mine cars and dead horses.

All along Slant No. 2, dazed men groped their way towards the surface, guided only by their intimate knowledge of the mine and the feeble light from their lamps. From time to time, they stumbled over the dead bodies of fellow miners.

Bill Guthrow, like most of the men in Level 1 North, realized that there had been an explosion, but had no conception of its magnitude. His first instinct was to reach the surface before he met the blackdamp. In his frantic race to freedom, Guthrow caught his boot in a mine track switch and was unable to free himself. His life was probably saved by Moorehouse coming up the slope and stopping to help. Guthrow whipped out his pocket knife and cut the heavy boot from his foot. Then he rejoined the men who were struggling towards safety before the gas overcame them.

Peter Dujay was working close to the bottom of Slant No. 2, some 2,400 feet from the entrance. Though he heard nothing, he was suddenly aware of a concussion and started up the long slope. A short distance along the incline he was joined by Engineer Hutchinson and his brother who were coming out of Level 3 South.

The Hutchinson brothers had been opening that section of the mine for ventilation and were the only two men on that level. Like Dujay, neither had heard the explosion but had felt a sudden rush of air, accompanied by falling rock. Knowing that something had happened, they followed the first law of mining and made for the surface.

As the three men started up Slant No. 2 they encountered brown coal smoke so dense that it rendered their lamps almost useless. They knew then that there had been an explosion or fire and that they would certainly encounter blackdamp ahead. Without oxygen masks, their chances of survival were slender. As they made their way up the slope they could sense other men moving near them, but they did not stop.

Evidence of destruction increased as they approached the entrance to Level 1 South. At the entrance they came across the bodies of Rod Wallis and William Neath, the Nova Scotians who on Monday would have been returning to their farm. They now lay dead beneath massive mine timbers. Finally, the brothers stumbled from the mine mouth, gasping for air and collapsing on their knees. At once, the frantic crowd of waiting women and children pressed forward to the rescued miners, presenting a danger almost as great as that of the mine itself.

It was a pathetically small group of eighteen men who finally emerged into the glaring sunlight. Of the 235 miners who had gone down, 217 were still trapped in the explosion-wracked, gas-laden tunnels. As the shocked survivors looked at each other, they began to realize that only a miracle could save any of the men still trapped in the shattered tunnels.

One of the rescued, David Murray, scrutinized the coal-blackened faces of the men around him. He saw that none of his three sons, Robert, William, or David Jr., was among them. "Where are my three boys?" he asked.

"They're still down the mine."

Before any one could stop him, he had wheeled and raced back to the mine entrance.

Constable Hancock, realizing Murray's intentions, grabbed him as he was about to enter the gas-filled corridors. The two men struggled briefly. Murray managed to throw the constable aside and disappeared into the darkness. Neither he nor his sons ever again saw daylight.

HURRY, HURRY, HURRY

With almost super-human strength, spurred by the knowledge that even seconds could mean the difference between life and death for those below, men clawed barehanded at the 8-inch blocks of concrete that choked the hoist engine. Under the cool direction of Mine Manager John Brown, whose two brothers were unaccounted for, they cleared the hoist, the tracks and righted a workable mine cart. Almost at the same moment that the frantic father, David Murray, broke loose from Constable Hancock and fled into the chaos, the first rescue car was ready. Among those who rode the first car into danger was Engineer Hutchinson who only moments before had himself emerged, almost overcome by gas and exhaustion.

The first crew, working without oxygen masks, was able to penetrate to the junction of Level 1 North and Level 1 South. Beneath the fallen timbers which blocked the entrance to Level 1 South, they found the bodies of Rod Wallis and William Neath. Pushing into Level 1 North, they heard the labored breathing of three men and passed them back to the mine car which whisked them to the surface, together with the bodies of Wallis and Neath. It was now 10 a.m. and the government rescue car had arrived from Blairmore in charge of D.S. Hyslop, who brought the welcome news that nearly 100 miners also were on their way. Among supplies on the rescue car were oxygen masks which were rushed to the mine entrance. At the same time, an emergency tent hospital was set up in the mine yard under Dr. William Dodd of the Hillcrest Hospital.

With the masks, Hutchinson and his party were able to push deeper into Level 1 North. Within minutes they brought another group of men overcome by blackdamp to the surface. They found the entrance to Level 1 South blocked with fallen debris, but managed to force their way through twisted track and smashed mine cars. Inside they found thirty men face down in water. All were dead.

Farther down Slant No. 2, another group of rescuers cleared debris from the second level. Almost at once their heroic efforts were rewarded. They came upon a group of survivors.

"I was working some distance inside No. 2 South," said Joseph Atkinson, one of the first rescued. "I didn't hear the report of the explosion. It was just as if I had suddenly gone deaf, or as if two 4-inch nails had been driven into my ears. That's how it felt. I was bowled over by the shock but scrambled to my feet."

The shock of the blast was followed by a wave of brown smoke,

Shocked families waiting on the hillside in an all-too-often vain hope that a husband, son or brother would emerge alive.

coming from Slant No. 1. It drove Atkinson and his fellow workers back. Sensing that the explosion had taken place in that vicinity, they turned and raced towards Slant 2. They found one miner on hands and knees groping along the corridor and tried to carry him but already deadly gases had invaded that section of the mine. They had to drop him and stagger on. Before they could reach the entrance to Slant No. 2, they encountered a solid wall of deadly blackdamp that drove them back.

"We lay down and rolled back with what strength we had left to a pool of water about 50 or 60 feet back, and there we crawled into the water, soaking our shirts and sucking them to keep off the effects of the afterdamp."

Gustaf Franz, unable to keep his head from falling into the water, was drowned. One by one the men fell unconscious. Atkinson's last recollection was of seeing a short distance away the body of a miner cut almost in two by the blast.

It was this group of men that Engineer Hutchinson found and brought to the surface. They were rushed to the hospital tent and given oxygen. All revived.

Hutchinson, meanwhile, returned to the mine. Although the intricate network of tunnels and passageways caused confusion as to where the explosions had occurred, it became apparent that the initial explosion had taken place near Level 1 South and No. 1 Slant. Here the greatest destruction had occurred. Between Slant 1 and Slant 2, however, the smoke and rushing air wound through the tunnels in such weird and confusing patterns that men trying to read the danger signals ran towards death rather than away from it. One group of nearly fifty men who escaped death from the initial blasts groped their way towards the entrance to Mine No. 1 only to find their exit blocked. There they were overtaken by blackdamp as they turned and tried to make their way back to Slant No. 2. All died.

Some were more fortunate. "I was working some distance in from the mouth of Slant No. 2 when the explosion occurred," said Herbert Yeadon. "It sounded somewhat like the discharge of a big gun on a battleship."

On coming out of the tunnel where he was working, Yeadon saw two men lying dead in a passageway leading to Slant No. 2. When moments later he saw men running towards him from that direction, he assumed that the explosion had taken place near Slant No. 2 and that the men were running from it. He, with several nearby miners, turned and ran towards Slant No. 1.

A short distance from Yeadon's tunnel, the fleeing miners encountered blackdamp and turned back, frantically searching for pools of water into which they could dip their clothing. By breathing through their wet clothes and sucking in the water they could obtain sufficient oxygen to sustain life. Believing that the center of the explosion was in Slant No. 2, their only hope lay in being found by rescue workers.

One by one the men round Yeadon lapsed into unconsciousness. Some never awakened, others were restored to life on hospital cots while anxious friends and relatives watched over them.

Meanwhile, in Level 1 North which had almost completely escaped the force of the explosions and where the exhaust fans had cleared the air, rescue work proceeded rapidly. Within an hour the last of the miners in that section had been brought to the surface alive.

By 11:30 a.m., forty men had either escaped under their own power or been brought out unconscious. With every passing moment, however, the pall of horror deepened around the mine entrance. Men, women and children slowly accepted the fact that only a series of miracles could help the remaining 198 men assumed to be in the death pit.

Two miracles did occur.

The first was the discovery by Robert Hood of the two brass checks he had absent-mindedly hung on their hooks early that morning. The two men he had sent home were safe. Their safety reduced the probable casualty list to 196, a figure that was announced publicly and appeared in early editions of many newspapers.

Shortly after 11:30 a.m., a squad of rescuers, under the direction of the indefatigable Hutchinson, fought its way through the debris of Level 1 South and discovered Herbert Yeadon and his companions. Only Yeadon and six others showed signs of life. They were rushed to the surface where all seven survived.

By 12 noon, miracles had ceased. Of the 235 men who had gone down the mine that morning, only forty-six remained alive, some of them barely breathing. Of the 189 others, the bodies of only twenty-six had been brought to the surface. Among them was David Murray, the father who had escaped but plunged back into the devastation in an effort to find his three sons.

Although a number of men had been rescued, Engineer Hutchinson was the only one with sufficient knowledge of the mine workings to give any clear picture of what had happened. Fireboss John Ironmonger was still unconscious; fireboss Sam Charlton was unaccounted for; Mine Superintendent James S. Quigley, pit boss Thomas Taylor, and other men who had intimate knowledge of the mine were still missing. From the information sent back by Hutchinson, a picture of conditions around Slant No. 2 was formed, but nothing was known about Slant No. 1.

A work crew was organized to unblock the choked throat of the rock tunnel and finally a hole was cleared large enough for one man to crawl through. Selected was Harry White, a former fireboss who had arrived with the rescuers from the other mines. Wearing an oxygen helmet and carrying spare oxygen on his back, he wormed his way through the narrow opening and dropped to the floor of Slant No. 1.

Men, horses, timber and mine cars were strewn in a chaotic mass. Mine tracks had been torn loose and bent into grotesque shapes. Between the mouth of the mine and Level 1 South, White counted the bodies of twenty-six men, some horribly disfigured by the explosion. Some, like Thomas Bardsley, had been transfixed in death — crouching, kneeling, walking. All had their lamps blown away.

As he approached tunnel 32, the evidence of destruction became greatest. From tunnels 31 to 35, the miners had been badly burned and disfigured.

There he found fireboss Sam Charlton, the firing cable still wrapped around his body. The battery was lying a few feet away, but the key necessary to activate the battery was missing. Later it was found in Charlton's pocket, and the two unexploded charges discovered in tunnel 32.

In the next tunnel, 33, the signs of destruction were the most obvious. White concluded that something had taken place in 33 that had made Sam Charlton hesitate and withhold detonating the charges in 32.

Later, Engineer Hutchinson arrived at the same conclusion after his examination of 33. Fireboss Daniel Briscoe, however, was equally positive that the explosion had originated a little farther along the Level, somewhere between tunnels 35 and 45. Whatever the point of origin, the devastation was so severe that no indication of the cause was clear. The only definite conclusion was that it could not have been caused by Sam Charlton.

Pushing his way through the cave-ins and rock falls, White came across thirty bodies — victims of blackdamp. They were in a side tunnel scarcely 50 feet from the blocked entrance to the mine.

It was a disheartening report that he made to Manager John Brown. He had seen no signs of life in any of the sections of the mines north of Slant No. 1. The only encouraging aspect was his discovery that severe though the explosion had been, there were no fires burning.

IDENTIFYING THE DEAD

Even under ideal conditions the Hillcrest Mine property was not pretty. The mountainside looked as if some mad barber had shaved clean the area around the mine entrance, leaving a stubble of blackened tree trunks. The once-brown soil was stained charcoal by the constant rain of coal dust, and the once-white rocks jutting from the stripped slopes were ugly black smudges. When RNWMP Inspector Christen Junget arrived from Pincher Creek at 11:30 a.m. to take charge of police operations, the scene resembled Dante's Inferno.

Dazed women, frightened children tagging at their heels, wandered aimlessly or sat dejectedly on coal-soiled mine equipment, unconscious of the damage to their clothing. When anyone came out of the mine, they rushed forward for a glimpse of what the mine car carried — perhaps a breath of information, of hope. Sadly, there was only despair.

After a brief consultation with mine officials, Inspector Junget relieved Corporals Grant and Mead and detailed them to the washhouse, replacing them with Corporal Searle and Constable Stanley Kistruck. Constable Hancock was assigned to collecting evidence for identification.

Six gangs of rescuers were at work in the mine, but their progress was slow. Only the men killed instantly were at their stations. The others had swarmed through the passages, vainly trying to find a way out of the deadly labyrinth. Each nook and cranny had to be searched, and many of the tunnels were sealed off with fallen rock or timbers.

The bodies of twenty-six men already brought up were carried to the washhouse and placed in charge of Mead and Grant. With a group of miners assisting, they washed the bodies and searched clothing for identification tags. In many instances the men were so disfigured that identification was impossible.

As the afternoon deepened, order was restored out of the tragic chaos. The grief-stricken crowds left the mine yard and gathered around the washhouse and the Miner's Hall. Only then did the most difficult part of the rescue work begin. Despite the anxious women and children waiting at the mine entrance, the rescuers had deliberately left many of the most badly mangled bodies inside, fearful lest the dismembered corpses unnerved the survivors. As the crowd thinned, they began to bring up parts of bodies and hastily sent the pieces into the concrete washhouse where the police tried to match bodies and limbs.

As the rescuers probed deeper into the mine, braving the continual danger of another explosion, they came upon small groups of men huddled around small pockets of water, all victims of blackdamp. When they were brought to the surface, the gas had to be pressed from them —

usually in the washhouse — and after a few hours the smell of gas hovered constantly inside the walls. Fortunately, Inspector Junget was a man of discernment, and a bottle of whiskey appeared on one of the shelves. It was a rather miraculous bottle that never seemed to run completely dry.

By dusk all realized that none of the remaining men below were alive.

One more person was almost added to this sad statistic. Robert Levitt, a miner who had arrived with the rescue crew from Bellevue, had gone into the mine without an oxygen mask, relying on the fans that had restored much of the air. Alone, he had ventured up a passageway to search for victims. When he tried to find his way back through the unfamiliar tunnels, he became lost and encountered a pocket of blackdamp. When the other members of the search party noted his absence and started a search, they found him unconscious. On the surface he lay near death for half an hour before the pulmotor revived him.

When darkness fell, all remaining hope for those below was officially given up. Under cover of night, Constable Hancock moved into the mine to search for missing legs and arms.

At 11:30 one of the rescue parties came across a fire burning in the mine. All crews were immediately recalled and placed on stand-by while a fire fighting party went below. When the fire was quelled the miners moved through the tunnels methodically searching for victims. One of the men encountered a pile of mine timbers and saw by the light of his lamp six or seven men dead in an alcove. Unable to reach them he could only mark the place for a later attempt.

In the washhouse, Corporals Mead and Grant worked steadily, their senses numbed by the horror of their task. As bodies were cleaned and assembled, they were wrapped in white shrouds and placed in wagons. Under the escort of other constables they were taken to the Miner's Hall and laid out in rows. When the Miner's Hall was filled, the upper story of George Cruickshank's General Store was requisitioned.

There had never been any feeling of goodwill between the miners and the police, but as the miners watched the three police officers work hour after hour without food, rest or relief, an official of the United Mine Workers Union said: "We have no use for the police, but we cannot help respecting its members when we see them working under such trying conditions."

Alert to the possibility of trouble if general drinking were allowed, Inspector Junget had the local hotel's licence suspended. The whiskey bottle on the shelf in the washhouse, however, continued to reproduce discreetly and promptly.

At 3 a.m. the rescue teams were again removed from the tunnels when a search team discovered another fire deeper in the mine. When it seemed that the mine was doomed a call came for more fire-fighters. In spite of the possible danger of another explosion from flames skipping along the ribbons of methane gas and encountering a pocket of gas, more men went into the mine. They were too tired to be heroes. They just wanted to finish their gloomy task.

The fire was brought under control just before dawn. Then the rescue teams, most of them without sleep for twenty-four hours, resumed their

Some of the dead awaiting interment in one of three mass graves. The largest, below, was some 200 feet long with the miners buried in two rows.

search of the underground spider web for more victims.

By Saturday noon, 162 bodies had been viewed by a Coroner's jury of ten miners and passed for burial. Still other segmented bodies were awaiting completion in the washhouse. The underground searchers had reached the destruction ridden section around tunnels 32 and 33 in Old Level 1. Here their progress was slow. There were fewer bodies and more fragments.

THREE HUGE GRAVES

Sunday, June 21, 1914, dawned cold and blustery. Dense white mists rolled over the valley floor between Hillcrest and Bellevue, while a chilling wind whipped snow flakes into the faces of men completing the last of three huge graves. Even as the first light filtered through the windows, people were stirring. Some slipped away to the Miner's Hall or Cruickshank's Store for a last look before the coffins were nailed shut. Others harnessed horses to carts, wagons and democrats for use as hearses. Still others merely sat and stared blankly into the uncertain future.

Under the supervision of the undertaker the coffins were laid out in rows on a vacant lot next to the General Store. Among those who passed was Fernand Capron, a twelve-year-old boy who had arrived from Belgium only the day before. As his father guided him between rows of coffins with their grieving attendants, he said: "Son, take note of this and never go down the mines."

At 10 a.m. funeral services began, Father Beaton officiating for Roman Catholics and Reverend Watkins for Anglicans. When they were completed, the hearses moved forward. With the Bellevue Band playing Saul's Dead March, the little procession started down the winding road and disappeared into the mist-shrouded valley. Then at 1 p.m. Union services began under the auspices of Reverend Young, assisted by eight other ministers. As the coffins were loaded onto the waiting wagons, the crowds around Cruickshank's Store diminished. Finally the vacant lot was empty of people and coffins.

As if the somber funeral processions were not enough, a macabre touch was added when a team of horses bolted, dumping their load of coffins by the roadside. Some of the wood caskets burst open, spilling the bodies on the ground. The mourners, already numbed by the terror of the past three days, quickly restored order and moved on towards the waiting mass graves.

By nightfall, 150 men had been laid to rest in the cemetery at the foot of Turtle Mountain. In the following days, the remains of Williams Fines, Fred Bennett and Herbert Adlam were placed in the hillside cemetery at Blairmore. Rod Wallis, William Neath and the bodies of four other miners were escorted to Nova Scotia by Andrew Wallis and his sister. Transportation was given without charge by the Canadian Pacific Railway as far as Saint John, New Brunswick, then the Intercolonial Railway carried them to their respective towns.

Scarce a day passed in the following two weeks that was not marked by a small funeral cortege along the winding road to the cemetery.

The bulk of miners who lost their lives were married — an estimated

130 left widows and most had children. Mine Superintendent James Quigley and David Walker each left a wife and six children. Charles Elick left a youthful family, the youngest born the day after the tragedy. In all, some four hundred children, most under ten, were made fatherless by the tragedy.

The families of those killed were entitled to $1,800 compensation from Hillcrest Collieries. Processing claims took time, however, and the need for immediate help was pressing. A local relief committee was formed, with a relief centre opened in Hillcrest. Relief offices were established in most cities of the Canadian West and various city councils voted grants to the stricken families. In addition, from the Federal

The grave of Dave Murray and his three sons. Murray was one of the few miners rescued but when told that his sons were still in the mine plunged back into the gas-filled tunnels. He died trying to find them.

government came a grant of $50,000 and from the province of Alberta another $20,000.

In the meantime, Corporals Mead and Grant with Constable Hancock had completed their grim task of identifying bodies. For a week they lived, ate and slept in the washhouse with its continuous parade of mangled bodies. Once the majority of bodies had been recovered, they spent hours searching the workings with miners, trying to locate parts of bodies and pieces of personal property. In many areas of the mine the debris still prevented proper search, but within a week after the maelstrom of death all but two bodies had been recovered.

In recognition, all three men were awarded a special sum of $50 for their courageous work. Constable Hancock, who earned 60 cents a day, was awed by this bonus of almost three months pay. Promotions for all followed shortly.

On July 7, 1914, a rescue team found one of the still missing miners.

He was Joseph Oakley, identified by the brass tag in his pocket. There remained only one brass check still unaccounted for in the timekeeper's office — that of Sidney Bainbridge. Years later, a retired Constable Hancock supplied the story of the missing miner.

Many of the bodies brought from the mine were without arms, legs or heads. The three policemen had striven valiantly to match limbs to torsos but, finally, one leg remained. The obvious conclusion was that Sidney Bainbridge had caught the full force of the blast and all that remained of his body was one leg. Without drawing undue attention, the police officers slipped the extra leg into one of the coffins and sealed it. Thus, one coffin bore the remains of two miners.

An official enquiry into the disaster revealed considerable disagreement about the cause of the explosion. All the firebosses affirmed that the Hillcrest workings were relatively safe — having neither an unusual amount of gas nor coal dust. By contrast, District Inspector of Mines Francis Aspinall testified that in his opinion the mine was both gaseous and dusty. Some witnesses stated that the explosion could have been caused by a pick throwing sparks from a rock; others felt that such sparks would be insufficient to start a fire. Lost in all the words was the quiet testimony of Harry White, the first man to traverse the mine from end to end while the ravages of the blast were still fresh.

In White's opinion, the explosion had occurred in tunnel 33 when sparks from a rock fall ignited the ever present methane gas. This fire resulted in the subsequent deadly explosion of coal dust. His theory was ignored. Twelve years later, however, he was to be vindicated.

Samples of coal dust from the mines had been submitted to the U.S. Bureau of Mines in Washington for testing. In his final report on October 24, 1914, Commissioner A.A. Carpenter stated that the dust from the mines was of a very high explosive nature. As a result, Carpenter reported that a gas explosion of unknown origin had triggered a coal-dust explosion, or several explosions.

Earlier, on July 23, a Coroner's jury at Coleman had rendered a verdict in which they stated that they did not think the Company had adhered strictly to the regulations of the Coal Mines Act. The jury also criticized the government Mine Inspection Branch for not inspecting mines more frequently, and the Safety Committee of the Hillcrest Mine Union for not having adequate safety apparatus on hand in case of accident.

Whatever the various verdicts and opinions, one tragic fact remained — 189 men died in the most terrible explosion in the history of Canadian mining.

THE YEARS AFTER

The evening of September 19, 1926, was light and warm as fireboss Frank Lote left the mine office and descended into Hillcrest Mine through the rock tunnel. Below in the clustered houses of the village 150 men were making final preparations to climb the hill and start the night shift. Following the 1914 disaster, improved mining methods and more modern safety apparatus had eliminated the cause of the first coal-dust explosions. With every fatality-free year the feeling of safety and security grew. But only a miracle on this day prevented upwards of 150 more miners dying from a massive explosion or the deadly blackdamp.

Frank Lote completed his rounds in the lower depths and started along Level 6 South which would bring him to Slant No. 2. Here the only other man in the mine, Fred Jones, was tending the pumping system between Levels 2 and 3 South.

It was 10:20 p.m.

Somewhere in the depths of the mine, rocks fell from a tunnel roof, struck sparks and ignited the methane gas. The flame skipped along the timbers and struck coal dust.

A thunderous explosion came from behind Frank Lote, killing him instantly. Even as billows of brown smoke cascaded over his inert form, the deadly fingers poked through the labyrinth of passageways seeking other victims. A surge of air rushed up Slant No. 2, bowling Fred Jones over and knocking his safety lamp from his head.

Within minutes a rescue party was formed at the mine entrance by Mine Inspector M. Johnson. Equipped with the latest safety devices, the men plunged into the smoke shrouded wreckage. On every side they saw that the explosion had caused greater devastation than the 1914 explosion. Timbers were blasted to pieces, mine cars crunched and iron rails twisted like threads of silk. This time, fortunately, they were looking for two men, not 235.

They found Fred Jones some 900 feet down the slope of Slant No. 2, his body limp, overcome by blackdamp. But it was three days before they discovered the clue to Frank Lote's whereabouts. While gangs of miners worked around the clock to repair the damage to the mine's interior, the rescue party found Lote's lamp lying in a pool of water in No. 6 Level South.

This time the evidence was clear. No spark from a miner's pick, no sudden flaring of a lamp, no unwise blasting had caused this upheaval. The only cause remaining was a rock fall. Those who had listened to Harry White's quiet testimony at the inquiry into Canada's worst disaster in 1914 wondered if the miner had been right after all. If so, no amount of safety precautions would ever render Hillcrest Collieries safe. Nothing could guarantee that in the miles and miles of mine workings rock would not fall, or that the mine would be empty when they did.

Nevertheless, within a month the mine was again functioning. Bratticemen roved the dark passageways directing the flow of air through the workings, miners dug and firebosses blasted, and carpenters hammered away in the bowels of Hillcrest Mountain. The days grew into months, the months into years. Finally, on December 1, 1949, the historic old mine closed because it was no longer competitive.

Charges of dynamite sealed forever the rock tunnel and the dirt entrance to Mine No. 2. The formidable tipple that overlooked the village of Hillcrest was torn down and transported to other mines in the area. Mine cars, tracks and machinery were removed to serve other mines or other purposes. With the passage of the years the roofs of the engine room and the washhouse caved in.

Today, nothing remains.

IN MEMORIUM

Ackers, Peter
Adlam, Herbert
Albenese, Dominic
Albenese, Nicholas
Anderson, Robert
Andreaschuk, Jacob
Androski, George
Armstrong, James
Bainbridge, Sidney
Banlant, Andrew
Banyar, Steve
Barber, James
Bardsley, Thomas
Bennett, Fred C.
Bingham, Fred
Bodio, Virgilio
Bolinski, John
Botter, Etalleredo
Bostock, Frank M.

Bowie, John S.
Bozzer, Pietro
Bradshaw, James
Brown, John
Brown, Thomas W.
Brown, William
Buckman, Albert
Camarda, Joseph
Cantalline, Peter
Carelli, Antonio
Carr, Henry
Cassagrande, Carlo
Cataline, Sam
Catanio, Antonio
Caterino, Basso
Celli, Vito
Chabillon, Emil
Chabillon, Leonce
Charles, Charles S.
Charlton, Sam

Ciccone, Eugenio
Cimetta, Antonio
Clarke, John
Clarke, Leonard
Coan, Charles
Corkill, Thomas
Coulter, Fred
Coulter, Robert
Court, Thompson
Cullinen, Dan
Daye, Prosper
Davidson, John
Demchuk, George
Demchuk, Nicholas
Dickenson, Matthew
Dugdale, Andrew
Dugdale, Robert
Elick, Charles
Emery, David
Eveloir, Everard
Ewing, James
Fedoruk, Peter
Fines, William
Flourgere, August
Fogale, John C.

Fortunato, Luigi
Fortunato, Vincenzo
Foster, John
Fox, William
Francz, Gustaf
Frech, Frank
Gallimore, William
Garine, Emil
Gasperion, Antonio
Gianoli, Carlo
Gramacci, Antonio
Gray, James F.
Guido, Ylio
Hansford, Ralph
Harris, David G.
Heber, John
Heusdens, Alphonse
Hicken, George
Hillman, William
Hnacnuk, Philip
Hood, John
Hunter, Hugh
Iluk, Wasyl
Ironmonger, Charles
Ironmonger, Sam

This Hillcrest soccer team illustrates the devastating effect of the disaster on the community.
Nine of the team were down the mine when the explosion occurred. Seven died.

BACK ROW
Frank Bostack (Killed)
M. Dickenson (Killed)
W. Rochester (Killed)
Thomas Dugdale
W. Miller (Killed)
Unknown face
R. Dugdale (Killed)
H. Jepson
Mr. Fisher
J. Moorehouse (Survivor)

FRONT ROW
W.G. Miller (Killed)
Jock Dugdale
H. Varley (Survivor)
W. Kyle
Wm. Fines (Killed)

nego, Mike	Morley, William	Pearson, John	Skurhan, Mike
hnson, Carl	Moore, William	Penn, James	Smith, Robert
hnson, Fred	Morrison, Alex	Penn, Robert	Smith, Thomas
hnson, William	Morron, Nick	Petrie, Alex	Somotink, Peter
ne, Pat	Mudrik, John	Petrie, James	Southwell, Albert
nock, Peter	Muir, Robert	Petrie, Robert	Stretton, Edward
pryanchuk, Mike	Muirhouse, Fred	Porteous, Alex	Tamborini, Albert
har, Petro	Murray, David sr.	Porteous, James	Tamborini, Baldo
smik, Chris	Murray, David jr.	Pounder, George	Taylor, Thomas
stynuk, Dan	Murray, William	Quigley, James S.	Thaczuk, John
rigatz, Fred	Murray, Robert	Quigley, Thomas	Thomas, Deo
zenko, Nick	Myrovich, Steve	Raitko, Steve	Trump, William
vasnico, Fred	McIssac, Rod	Ralnyk, Bernard	Turner, Thomas
vasnico, Wasyl	McKay, Angus H.	Ralnyk, Fred	Turner, William
bonne, Frank	McKinnon, John B.	Rees, Albert	Tyron, Mike
gard, Antoine	McKinnon, Steve	Robertson, George	Vendrasco, Fred
elanchuk, Steve	NcNeil, Pius	Rochester, Joseph H.	Vohradsky, Joseph
archetto, Ulderico	McQuarrie, John A.	Rochester, William	Vohradsky, Vince
arcolli, Guiseppi	Neath, William	Rossanese, Eugenio	Walker, David J.
egency, Nicholas	Oakley, Joseph	Rosti, Luigi	Wallis, Rod
eiklejohn, Adam	Pagnan, Eduardo	Sands, John	Wilson, Thomas L.
elok, John	Pardegtt, Arthur	Sandul, John	Zahara, John
ller, William	Parnisari, Carlo	Sandulik, Daniel	Zamis, Luis
ller, William G.	Parnisari, Guiseppi	Schroeder, Charles	Zapisocki, Wasyl
ontelli, Dominic	Payet,Leon	Silva, Alfred	Zaska, Michael

FERNIE: CITY UNDER A CURSE

The city of Fernie is a prosperous and tranquil-looking community of some 7,000 amid snowy peaks in the B.C. section of the Crowsnest Pass. Its tranquil appearance is misleading, however, since its history records more tragedies than any other community in the Pass, a region where disaster has struck frequently and brutally. While other Crowsnest communities such as Bellevue, Hillcrest, Frank and Coleman have escaped with one major calamity, Fernie has experienced a series. They range from mine explosions, one alone killing 128 men, to fires, the worst a conflagration that left virtually all 6,000 residents homeless.

While the general reasons for these disasters point to man's carelessness or nature's excesses, there are those who blame the "curse" for the disasters that have befallen the community. According to legend, the curse originated when a group of men were prospecting for minerals near

Crowsnest Mountain. Among them was William Fernie, after whom the community is named. One night prior to the 1890s when the prospecting group was camped beside an Indian band, Fernie noticed that the Chief's daughter was wearing a necklace of shiny black stones. He recognized them as pieces of coal. Thwarted in his effort to find their source, he wooed the Indian girl and learned her secret. Then he deserted her. In great anger her mother invoked a curse on the Elk River Valley and all its inhabitants "who will suffer from fire, flood, strife and discord; all will finally die from fire and water!"

Whether the story of the widely believed curse was of Indian or white invention is not known, nor whether Fernie was the unfaithful Romeo. The latter is highly unlikely, however, since in the Crowsnest Pass coal wasn't

Travelling faster than a galloping horse, in less than two hours Fernie's 1908 conflagration not only engulfed the Catholic church, below, but also destroyed over 1,000 other buildings. Only twenty-three houses remained, leaving 6,000 residents homeless.

hidden or hard to find. It was, in fact, so common that prospectors searching for gold complained about "coal, coal, everywhere." So much was evident that the region was christened "nature's coal bin."

If there is doubt about Fernie's involvement with the curse, there is none about another aspect of his life. He was among the first to begin systematically prospecting for coal and one of a group which in 1889 organized the Crow's Nest Coal and Mineral Company. It received a charter to build a railway through the Pass and in 1897 made an arrangement with the Canadian Pacific Railway which in 1898 built the B.C. Southern. The original Crow's Nest Coal and Mineral Company changed its name to Crow's Nest Pass Coal Company and began large-scale mining. Fernie later sold his interest and moved to Victoria. If there was a curse he wasn't affected. He lived to be eighty-four and left an estate of nearly $300,000, a huge fortune for the times.

The Crow's Nest Pass Coal Company grew quickly. Their 250,000 acres of land west of the Elk River contained over eighty seams of coal, enabling them to produce varying grades — blacksmithing, coking, bituminous, steam and semi-anthracite. By the end of 1897 the firm had opened No. 1 tunnel on the north side and No. 2 tunnel on the south side of Coal Creek. Situated five miles from the Elk River, the mines were in a narrow valley bounded by steep hills that virtually blocked the winter sun, with avalanches always a threat.

Headquarters of the company was at Fernie, a CPR station on the flats bordering Elk River where 200 beehive-shaped coke ovens were built, as well as a branch rail line to the mines at Coal Creek. Not far from the ovens two rows of shacks "of unbarked logs" were the first buildings in what would be "Old Fernie."

Within a year the townsite of Fernie was laid out across the CPR tracks. The new community grew quickly and in 1900 a Montreal writer who identified himself only as "W.B. McB." wrote:

"Fernie presents a remarkable example of the way western towns are built up. Three years ago what is now the site of the town was a dense forest of Douglas fir, cedar and spruce. In the following year a 'shack town' sprang up with the advent of the railway and commencement of mining activity. At that time it was wild and lawless, but presented splendid opportunities for making money.

"Now though only about two years old, it is a town of over 2,000 inhabitants with a park, athletic grounds, skating rink, four or five churches and several very good hotels. It is quite well supplied with modern conveniences, such as electric lights and waterworks, and there is a wide awake enterprising spirit about the place that seems strange to a steady-going easterner."

In December 1901 the *Fernie Free Press* reported with satisfaction:

"The population of Fernie today is 3,000, which entitles it to be regarded as the third largest town in the interior of the Province of British Columbia, Rossland coming first and Nelson second. At the present rate of progress Fernie will in the course of two years pass both; there is little doubt that this will be the case since there is no element of speculation in the mineral development of the town.

"With the program sketched out by the large corporation doing business here, it is not too much to expect that a few years will see Fernie with a population of 10,000, and a coal and coke industry of such dimensions as will place it ahead of any mineral camp in the Province."

Less than six months later the paper recorded the first in what would be a series of mine disasters. Like other mines in the Crowsnest Pass, Coal Creek was dangerous because of the gas and fine coal dust. The Montreal writer had been taken on a tour of the mine and wrote:

"When the gas is present in large enough proportions it gradually fills the room, and when ignited forms a solid mass of flame, and I have frequently seen men terribly burned by it though the fire lasted only a few seconds. Sometimes, too, it forms in such large quantities that when mixed with air it gives rise to violent explosions in which many lives are lost. At Salt Lake City, Utah, last summer 200 lives were lost. So far no lives have been lost in Fernie, in this way, which is rather remarkable, as open lights are used almost exclusively."

The mine's good fortune ended on May 22, 1902, when an explosion ripped through No. 2 mine with such force that "while funeral trains were assembled to take the bodies down to Fernie . . . some were so mangled that they were taken right to the burial ground." Of the disaster, the *Fernie Free Press* reported:

"About 7 o'clock on the evening of May 22, 1902, a cloud of smoke, gas and dust shot 1,000 feet into the air from the fanhouse on No. 2 mine, followed by a shrill unscheduled whistle from the Coal Creek plant. These marked an explosion in the depths of No. 2 and adjoining No. 3 mines which snuffed out the lives of 128 men, almost the whole working shift. Not a man out of the 90 employed in the shaft of No. 2 mine lived to tell the tale but in No. 3, 20 survivors had escaped from the left side of the slope. . . .

"Within twelve minutes rescuers were at hand but found that the pipes in the roof of the tunnel which conducted air throughout the mine had been destroyed. It was impossible to enter the mine until these were repaired. For six hours they worked, every few moments a man collapsing and another taking his place. About 2 a.m. they found the first body, Joe Sengala, and a moment later Stephen Morgan. Neither had any marks. At 4 a.m. work had to be suspended for several hours to let the gas escape. All day Friday the search continued. By 6 o'clock 31 had been taken out but a fall of rock delayed getting the last bodies for several days. Townspeople fell in behind the wagons carrying bodies to their graves while a newspaperman wrote: 'Fernie is in a condition of gloom and resounds with the hopeless cries of widows and orphans'."

Shortly after the 1902 explosion the first miners' strike occurred at Coal Creek Colliery when a new manager roused hostility by extending the day's work from 8 to 8½ hours. The strike lasted seven weeks but unfortunately for the miners, resulted in almost unconditional surrender.

The year 1902 also resulted in a near disaster when summer brought a serious outbreak of typhoid from polluted water. Fortunately, the disease was arrested when Fernie's water intake was changed from below the mine discharge to above.

A crew at the entrance to No. 2 mine at Coal Creek in 1902. All were in the mine during the devastating explosion. Only four survived.
Below is the railroad and business area of Fernie at the time of the 1902 mining disaster. Two years later a fire destroyed everything.

Two years later a fire devasted the community, wiping out almost the entire commercial center. It broke out in the early morning of April 30 in C. Richard's general store and by 8 a.m. the whole block was smoldering embers. But the community quickly recovered, the "embers had hardly cooled before the sound of carpenters' hammers were heard."

Fernie was incorporated as a city in July 1904, the first City Council passing many measures which they hoped would help prevent destructive fires. Among new buildings was one built by Crow's Nest Pass Coal Company, a massive stone office set well back from the street. Four years later when Fernie was engulfed by a massive conflagration the stone office was to be an oasis amid block after block of ashes.

Before then, however, there were a range of other disasters. The first was another major fire in 1905. It started in George Carruther's tailor shop, located in a room of the *Free Press* building, and destroyed a town block worth $80,000. J.R. Wallace, later owner and editor of the newspaper, slept above Carruther's shop and had a narrow escape. Waking from sleep he noticed flames coming up around the stovepipe. He grabbed his clothes and fled, picking up some galleys of type and a few other small items. That was all that was saved of the printing plant. A month later another block of wooden buildings burned, with damage this time some $40,000.

That same year two mine tipple buildings caught fire. Next morning nothing remained but hot ashes and twisted iron. While the destroyed tipple buildings were replaced by a single steel structure, the fire resulted in No. 3 mine being flooded. It remained closed for nearly four years.

In 1906 residents were free of serious fires but for those with relatives in the mines there was an ominous development. There occurred the first of many "bumps" which would become a deadly factor in subsequent disasters in Coal Creek mines. Technically, a bump is the coming together of roof and floor within a mine, probably due to geologic stress. At the time officials at Coal Creek could not pinpoint the cause.

For the next two years these bumps continued with no serious results. Then on July 31, 1908, a big bump in No. 2 mine at Coal Creek killed three miners and imprisoned twenty others for eight hours. Of the twenty, one who was taken out alive with no bodily injuries died later from shock. As a result of the deadly bump, all the shafts of the active area of No. 2 mine were abandoned.

Before shocked townspeople could bury the victims of the bump, a greater disaster unfurled. For ten days that July the town had been clouded with smoke from a bush fire burning in logging debris at the Cedar Valley Lumber Company's mill near West Fernie. It was not considered dangerous until a brisk wind sprang up about two o'clock on Saturday morning, August 1. The slash fire suddenly became a monster which wiped out the Cedar Valley mill, then a volcano of flame which advanced on Fernie. At the Dairy Ranch the flames split, one all-consuming tongue roaring eastward along the Great Northern Railway; the other to the west, its mass easily leaping the barrier of the Elk River. In West Fernie the fire department valiantly fought to check the blaze at the Elk Lumber Company which had 6 million feet of lumber in the yards.

The department's effort was futile. Mill and lumber became a massive inferno, the gale-force wind carrying embers and even burning lumber into the city.

The Fernie, Central and Waldorf Hotels were quickly blazing, as was the Opera House, its roof blown off and carried a block by the super-hot wind before the fire even reached it. Townspeople fled, many barely able to keep ahead of the flames. Later the *Free Press* noted that many survivors had been ". . . scorched and blistered by whirling flames, blinded by smoke, crazed by separation from loved ones and fleeing they knew not where, checked by walls of flame just as safety seemed at hand, confused by the suddeness of the catastrophe and faint with seemingly futile exertion!" People of Old Town, most of them foreigners, had to be driven toward the north by cool-headed men, the crying, screaming, mothers praying and carrying children. Two hundred people crowded into the stone office of the Crow's Nest Pass Coal Company, another sixty women and children took refuge in Western Canada Wholesale Warehouse, while men on the roof kept the shingles wet.

Without the Coal Company's office as a refuge, many of the 200 who found safety there would probably have died. As Mayor W.W. Tuttle remarked later: "A man on a horse couldn't have kept ahead of the fire."

One graphic account was written by a miner named William Richard Puckey who had a few hours previously helped remove one of the three miners killed by the bump at No. 2 mine. He left Coal Creek on the train and remembered:

The main business section of Fernie before the devastating fire in 1908.

"When we were within one mile of Fernie we came upon French Camp that was two rows of wooden houses, built along each side of the track. They were all ablaze together, and into that blazing hell the engineer dashed, with one coach and the flatcar with the reels on.

"I shouted, 'Put handkerchiefs over nose and mouth.' When we got through, the coach was all afire and the city was all on fire together.

"Men, women and children were fleeing in all directions, calling for help. The sight of it will never be forgotten by those who went through it all. One family in particular, a Mr. David Murray, wife and 10 children were leaving for the Old Home, Scotland. When we got to Fernie both Mr. and Mrs. Murray had lost their nerves. She threw five children through an open window and Mr. Murray pulled her through. Mr. Murray grabbed two boys and I got two more. Mrs. Murray got the little girl, then we called on the others to follow, and I rushed off, heading for the river.

"I hailed a passing team, and got them all piled on, and told the driver to drive to either station, the CPR or the GN. I then went to look for the others, but it was in vain. Fires were springing up all around us, the smoke was choking, and there were other women and children to save. . . .

"Great big trees were torn up as if by unseen hands, and the sun, when it pierced the clouds, shone down like a ball of fire. Fires sprang up wherever it shone for a second, but there happened to be two engines at the depot, and the crews soon had a line of empty box cars ready.

"Into these we packed all the women and children until we had about 30 (box cars) loaded. Then the fires were beginning to warm us up all around, and you could not see for smoke. Then we pulled out of the burning city, but on all sides of us fires were burning. After going about five miles, we got to a place where, to get the line level, they had cut away from the base of one of the mountains here.

"The train pulled up, and 1500 people rushed from the box cars to the river's edge. The river just here was about 300 feet wide so that from one side we were safe, but further along the track, we could see flames creeping up on three sides. . . ."

In ninety minutes Fernie had virtually vanished. That there were any buildings left at all was due to the efforts of volunteer firemen and the freak nature of the wind. The brewery was gone, the first building to be burned. So were Fernie's eleven hotels and everything belonging to the CPR — freight shed, coal chutes, freight and coal cars, two pullmans, a mile of track and the depot. Great Northern saved their station and water tank but coal cars in front of the depot were melted.

Every retail house in town was in ashes, as was the new post office, skating rink, four banks, school, two newspaper offices, and the brand new provincial building. In all, over 1,000 buildings were destroyed. Only twenty-three houses survived, leaving some 6,000 citizens homeless.

The only fortunate aspect of the holocaust was that as far as could be determined, only ten people died. The *Cranbrook Herald* on August 6, 1908, reported that the dead included "F. Ford, wife and children, of West Fernie, who were found in a well and the condition of the bodies shows they had actually been boiled. Mrs. Turner, of Fernie Annex. Lena

The devastation after the 1908 holocaust. At right center is the roof of the opera house, blown off and carried a block before the fire reached the building.
Within a year the courageous community had rebounded, below, its new buildings substantial ones of stone, concrete and brick.

Wood, a colored resident of the restricted district. Four foreigners found in Old Town, names unknown.''

In response to a telegraphed plea "City total loss, 6,000 homeless . . . need tents. . . . '' the neighboring community of Cranbrook had a train on the way in forty minutes. Spokane, Washington, had another train underway in just over one hour. The Cranbrook train arrived at midnight and exchanged its provisions and clothes for refugees. Every household in Cranbrook took them in, clothed and fed them. Money and supplies poured in from B.C. and elsewhere and citizens of Fernie responded with bravado and courage. An advertisement in the *Free Press* shows their spirit: "When the Smoke Clears Away, You Will Find Us Doing Business at the Old Stand." The paper itself was proof of the aid which poured into the devastated community. It suddenly found itself with a complete new printing plant, sent in unasked by a Winnipeg firm.

Within a year the city was virtually re-established. A 1910 report listed three sawmills, a foundry, brick factory, brewery, fifteen hotels, four cigar stores, one cigar factory, curling and skating rinks, three theatres, three banks, seven wholesale houses, five churches, six lodges, ten labor unions and two weekly newspapers.

The coal industry was healthy and in 1913 there was a record output at Coal Creek. Some 825,815 tons of coal were moved with 1,478 men employed. Population had risen to 5,000 and the harrowing fire faded into history.

Citizens, however, were still alert. The curse placed by the Indian woman threatened disaster by water as well as by fire. In 1911 there were anxious days when what was described as "the heaviest snowfall in living memory" stranded CPR passenger trains in Fernie. Food was getting scarce when relief trains finally punched through. While the heavy snow didn't cause any known deaths, the potential was always present. In December 1912 a massive rock and snow slide crashed onto Coal Creek mine, demolishing the carpenter and electrical shops and killing six men.

The winter of 1915-16 was another snow year, with over sixteen feet falling, in some places covering even the upper windows of houses. In previous years Fernie had often been swept by rampaging floods, forcing residents in low-lying Annex, Annex Extension and West Fernie to move to higher ground. The worst flood, however, occurred in the spring of 1916. Among other damage it washed away a bridge and the pipeline from Fairy Creek supplying the city's water. All summer long water for the town had to be supplied from the Coal Creek reservoir. Sydney Hutcheson recalls in his book, *The Curse,* that a gully ran diagonally across their backyard and there was two feet of water in their house.

During the townspeople's ordeals by floods and fire there had been no further disasters to miners. After the lethal bumps in mines No. 2 and No. 3 a new mine known as No. 1 East was opened in 1911 on the seam above. It became the most important one in the colliery's operation, with a new method of operation that made everyone hope that the problem of bumps had been resolved. Although the potentially deadly bumps still occurred, nearly all gave sufficient warning for workers to escape. One instance was in November 1916. A bump shook the surrounding countryside like an earthquake. It completely destroyed part of No. 1 East but caused no deaths.

Unfortunately, an explosion at No. 3 on April 5, 1917, was disastrous. There were thirty-four men underground. All died. One man was found alive at the foot of the slope but died later, bringing the total to thirty-five. Rescuers found the bodies badly burned and crushed or buried under massive rockfalls, one of which buried the mine locomotive and all eighteen cars it had been hauling.

After this disastrous explosion improvement of the ventilation system, introduction of a gas detector that would pick up lower percentages, electric safety lamps, spraying and rock-dusting of roadways brought ten years without any loss of life. During that time probably 200 blowouts had taken place without fatal injuries until August 30, 1928. Shortly before noon on that day an outburst of gas and coal in No. 1 East mine killed six miners.

Seven months later there was trouble again in No. 1 East. On March 25, 1929, indications of fire were noticed coming from a caved roadway in No. 1 East. Operations to remove the heated material started at once but progress was slow for the coal seam had been very thick and the roof had caved badly. Men were almost three weeks fighting their way to the fire. On April 12 a small explosion slightly burned two men. The next day a fall or slide took place above the fire and although everything had been saturated with water the fall was accompanied by coal-dust. It immediately exploded, seriously burning ten men. Luckily, no lives were lost.

Another ten-year interval of quiet followed the 1928 and 1929 outbursts. Then on September 20, 1938, a violent bump wrecked the main entry to the East slope. Four miners were seriously injured and three killed.

In addition to the series of mine accidents, the community had other difficulties. The early 1920s were marked by labor troubles and strikes, compounded in August 1923 when the Home Bank went broke, owing $800,000. Hundreds of residents lost their life savings.

Then came the Depression of the 1930s with the mines operating only two days a week. Nine out of ten families were on relief. The 1930s also resulted in another ominous development. Ever since 1904 the Great Northern Railway had provided a second rail line to the coal mines via Rexford, Montana, through Fernie to Michel. In 1926 the GNR abandoned its line between Elko and Michel, using CPR tracks for its daily train. In 1936 the GNR reduced service to a mixed passenger and freight train once a week. Then in 1938 the service was terminated, the rails from Elko to the U.S. border removed. Great Northern's withdrawal was a serious blow to Coal Creek mines for it had been the chief customer for many years.

Although World War Two brought increased demand for coal, when hostilities ended there was for Fernie a disastrous development. Railways increasingly replaced with diesel engines the coal burning locomotives which had sustained the Crowsnest Pass mines. In 1958, despite a newly installed $1.5 million steel tipple, Coal Creek mine was closed. Although it had yielded some 20 million tons of coal and could have kept producing, a changing civilization had relegated steam-powered trains to history books and coal-burning cook stoves and furnaces to museums.

"The closure will kill our city," lamented Fernie's mayor. "The mine employed 400 men. About thirty can find jobs in Michel but the rest will have to leave and then there won't be anyone left to pay the taxes."

The mayor's concern was well founded since even Michel was fated to disappear in a few years. Then someone remembered the curse invoked by the distraught Indian mother over sixty years previously. Certainly the Crowsnest Pass seemed to be under some type of bad omen. As predicted, residents had suffered ". . . fire, flood, strife and discord," and over 600 had perished. Perhaps they had now paid the penalty for the alleged wrong done to the Indian maiden so long ago; perhaps now the curse could be lifted.

Accordingly, when Highway 3A was opened in August 1964 Chief Big Crane of the Tobacco Plains Indians arrived from Montana. With him were forty members of his band, their purpose to lift the curse. They did so with a solemn ritual of song, chant and the throb of drums. Since then, fate has been kinder to Fernie.

A vast new market for coal developed in Japan, not for steam engines or home heating but for thermal and metallurgical use in steel mills. Demand grew year by year, with production soon surpassing the years from the early 1900s to the late 1940s when 1 million tons was considered exceptional. By contrast, in 1981 alone Westar Mining shipped over 7 million tons.

Because of this development Fernie's income rose from just over $15 million in 1971 to nearly $70 million in 1981. Today new schools and a hospital, senior citizen's housing, modern sub-divisions, a major ski development amid the spectacular Rocky Mountain scenery, curling rink, ice arena and nine-hole golf course enable her citizens to enjoy a blend of the modern and the historical. Much of the downtown area retains its heritage of 1908 when after the calamitous fire buildings were rebuilt of brick and stone.

For visitors, Fernie's Tourist Information Centre can provide information on these historic buildings and other local points of interest. One is the burning coal mine at Coal Creek, five miles from Fernie. When the seam caught fire is not known, though old-timers favor about 1916. The Fernie Historical Museum in the Roman Catholic Church Rectory, built in 1905, provides an excellent window to the past. In addition to items of historical interest from the district, the museum building has the original doors, kitchen cupboards, and some of the 1905 linoleum.

The museum is also a reminder that communities born with Fernie during the early 1900s — Coal Creek, Hosmer, Morrissey, Natal and Michel — have disappeared. Although Fernie on many occasions seemed fated to follow, she has not only survived but is today the largest community in the Crowsnest Pass.

THE CROWSNEST PASS TODAY

The Alberta communities of Frank and Hillcrest still survive, although not independently. Today they are part of the Municipality of Crowsnest Pass, formed when the mining communities of Bellevue, Hillcrest, Frank, Blairmore and Coleman amalgamated. They have a combined population of some 7,000 and extend for about 9 miles along Highway 3. They offer tourist

facilities from shopping malls to campgrounds, motels to a museum. In addition, there is the impressive Frank Slide Interpretive Centre and Leitch Collieries Provincial Historic Site, both administered by the Alberta government.

Leitch Collieries Historic Site is at the Alberta entrance to the Pass on Highway 3, west of the small community of Lundbreck. This site, once the location of an 1881 North-West Mounted Police outpost, was known as

The Frank slide dominates the eastern end of the Alberta section of the Crowsnest Pass.

CROWSNEST MOUNTAIN

BLAIRMORE

FRANK TODAY

FRANK SLIDE INTERPRETIVE CENTRE

FRANK (ORIGINAL LOCATION)

BELLEVUE

MAPLE LEAF (A BELLEVUE SUBURB)

Police Flats. Leitch Collieries was established near this old outpost in 1909. Here company president Malcolm Leitch and mine manager William Hamilton, with big dreams and expectations, built a large sandstone powerhouse, a coal washing plant which was the tallest building in the Pass, and 101 coke ovens. The ovens required over one million bricks, all imported from Pennsylvania.

Passburg was named by Mrs. Hamilton, the mine manager's wife, who envisaged it as the main city of the Pass. It was built on a plain just west of Leitch Collieries. Buildings included miners' houses, a school, a hotel and a general store. The adjacent mine manager's sandstone residence was the showpiece of the Pass, with running water, electricity, a dumbwaiter and a room for visiting church ministers. Unfortunately, Leitch Collieries, like most coal mines in the Pass, had a short life. The boom years didn't come soon enough, and the large capital outlay was never recovered. After eight years, Leitch Collieries closed its doors. While Passburg has disappeared except for a few foundations where buildings once stood, the sandstone walls of the mine manager's residence and the mine powerhouse still stand.

They, too, seemed fated to disappear. Fortunately, the Crowsnest Pass Historical Society convinced the Alberta government that the ruins were an important historical asset. As a result, they were designated a Provincial Historical Site. Ruins were stabilized and interpretive panels and listening posts installed. The rock-walled shell of the powerhouse is the main attraction, it and the other displays graphically portraying life in a typical mining community over eighty years ago. The site includes picnic facilities, washrooms and a large parking area. In summer daily guided tours are available.

After Leitch Collieries the next point of interest is the miniature Drive-In Chapel just off Highway 3 in Bellevue. Built by Chris Withage of Lethbridge who donated his labor, it has a seating capacity of eight and features recorded music and sermons. After the Frank Slide it is probably the most photographed attraction in the Crowsnest Pass.

Bellevue was born in 1901 as a result of nearby coal deposits. It, too, has known tragedy, the worst in 1910 when thirty men died in a coal mine explosion. In 1920 there were more deaths when two policemen were killed in a shootout with two robbers at the Bellevue Cafe. One of the robbers was killed, the second later captured and hanged. Bellevue today has a population of some 1,200 and a variety of visitor services, including a campground with full hook-ups and the cafe where the shootout occurred. (A complete account of the tragedy is in Heritage House book, *Outlaws and Lawmen of Western Canada, Volume Three*.)

In Bellevue a glimpse of the region's coal mining history is offered through a tour of the mine which operated from 1903 to 1961. A portion of the original tunnel has been opened to visitors with guided tours during the summer. To provide a geniune experience of working conditions, the only light comes from miners' lamps issued to visitors. Since the temperature in the mine is about 45°F, visitors should wear warm clothing and sturdy footwear. For current information phone Crowsnest Pass Ecomuseum Trust at (403) 562-8831.

Across the Crowsnest River from Bellevue is Hillcrest with its graveyard containing over 100 of the 189 miners killed in the 1914 explosion. Hillcrest is on the south side of Highway 3, the paved access road well marked. It is now a residential community of some 400 and the site of the annual Crowsnest Pass Rodeo. The graveyard is just opposite the rodeo grounds. An historical point of interest is the building where those killed in the 1914 disaster were placed prior to the mass funeral. Hillcrest is also the eastern terminus of the old road through the Frank Slide.

About 2 miles west of Bellevue is Frank, with the Frank Slide Interpretive Centre just over one-half mile north of Highway 3. From the Centre, Turtle Mountain dominates the skyline to the southeast; the slide fills the foreground; to the west are the communities of Blairmore and Coleman, and the landmark of Crowsnest Mountain; while eastward are Bellevue and Hillcrest. In the Centre, interpretive programs, display panels and an award winning audio-visual presentation, "In The Mountain's Shadow," tell not only the story of the Frank Slide but also the mining and social history of the Crowsnest Pass from the 1890s to the 1940s. In addition, a hiking trail about 1 mile long through the slide gives visitors a personal look at the destruction wreaked by this devastating avalanche of rock.

The Centre offers washrooms, picnic sites, a gift shop and a large parking area. It is open daily from 9:00 a.m. to 8 p.m. in summer; 10:00 a.m. to 4:00 p.m. in winter.

Like Hillcrest, Frank is largely a residential community of some 200. The site of the original town is now an industrial park, although a fire hydrant and the cellars of some of the original buildings of the early 1900s are still visible.

From Frank a road heads up Gold Creek Valley to the ghost town of Lille, although the 4-mile route is rough and a four-wheel drive vehicle is recommended. (Check at the Frank Slide Interpretive Centre for current conditions. Phone (403) 562-7388.)

Lille was born in 1901 when J. J. Fleutot and C. Remy of the British Columbia Gold Fields Company found promising seams of coal at the base of Grassy Mountain. They opened a mine, its primary purpose to supply coal to the Canadian Pacific Railway. A community first called French Camp, then Lille, grew around the mine. By 1907 population had reached 700, with services that included a hotel, school and fifteen-bed hospital. Unfortunately, as miners dug deeper into the mountain the quality of the coal deteriorated and expenses rose. As a consequence, the mine closed in 1913. Today the only signs of the community are indentations where once stood buildings and rows of crumbling coke ovens with expensive bricks specially imported from Belgium.

Just west of Frank on Highway 3 is Blairmore, born in 1903. With a population of some 2,400, it is the largest of the Alberta Crowsnest Pass communities. Its services include a wide variety of business places, swimming pool, golf course, museum, liquor store, RCMP headquarters, campground with full hook-ups and, for winter visitors, a ski hill, jump and other facilities.

Adjoining Blairmore to the west is Coleman. Born in 1904 as a result of rich coal deposits in the area, it has a population of about 1,400 and a wide variety of business places. In addition, it claims to possess "The World's Biggest Piggy Bank."

On Highway 3 in Coleman, the "Piggy" is used by the Coleman Lions Club as a fund raiser. A plaque has the following information:

"This is TEN TON TOOTS, known to miners as a 'Dinky'. Toots hauled five million tons of coal to daylight over 180,000 miles of underground tracks. Toots is a 7 x 7 x 14 compound air locomotive, using compressed air at 800 pounds pressure to pull up to 200-ton loads.

"Toots invites your inspection and contribution."

Another attraction in Coleman is the Crowsnest Museum which is a tribute to the Crowsnest Historical Society. As the Society notes: "Our general purpose is to collect, preserve and portray the heritage of the Crowsnest Pass and district through natural history specimens, artifacts, documents, maps, pictures and information which is significant to the history of the area."

The Museum is located in the former Coleman High School, a gracious brick building now over fifty years old. The Society purchased the building for $1 and with volunteer help turned it into a museum which represents the Alberta section of the Crowsnest Pass. The project is ongoing but completed projects include a room depicting a typical early commercial centre, complete with dentist's office, blacksmith's shop, general store and barber shop.

Another room depicts community life and includes a pioneer school and miner's cottage. A naval exhibit commemorates *HMCS Blairmore,* a minesweeper which formed part of the Royal Canadian Navy during World War Two. Upstairs, a fish and wildlife diorama depicts the region's wildlife heritage from streams through forest to alpine country.

Outside on the former school grounds is a large display of mining equipment which includes a rail bending kiln from Greenhill Mine and a model of a horse-drawn coal car. Also here are a park and rest area. The Museum is open from 10-12 a.m. and 1-4 p.m. during the summer and includes a gift shop. Phone (403) 563-5434.

At Coleman a prominent landmark is 9,138-foot Crowsnest Mountain, after which the Pass is named. There are many theories behind the mountain's name, including one that it stems from a battle between Crow and Blackfoot Indians. According to this version, the Blackfoot managed to trap marauding Crow Indians and killed them in a "nest" at the base of the mountain. They named the mountain Crows Nest to commemorate their victory.

The generally accepted origin of the name is that while it is Indian, it did not evolve from a slaughter. It is a translation of the Cree Indian name, *kah-ka-ioo-wut-tshis-tun,* and refers to the crows' nests in the trees at the base of the mountain. The first mention of the name by white men was made in 1858 by Lieutenant Thomas Blakiston, exploring the region to find the most southerly pass through the Rocky Mountains exclusively in British Territory.

Turtle Mountain and the Frank Slide from the
Alberta Government's Interpretive Centre.

The Drive-In Chapel at Bellevue and the
"World's Biggest Piggy Bank" at Coleman.

Over the years there have been many variations in the spelling of Crowsnest Pass, including Crow Nest, Crow's Nest and Crows Nest. The official way is Crowsnest, although local residents refuse to part with Crow's Nest.

Coleman is also the southern terminus of Kananaskis Highway 940, also known as the Forestry Trunk Road. From Coleman the Kananaskis (Can-an-as-kiss) heads northward 140 miles through the east slopes of the Rocky Mountains to the Trans-Canada Highway at Seebe, 55 miles west of Calgary. Many people consider it to be Alberta's most scenic drive. One-half of the route is paved, the rest gravel treated to control dust.

The highway cleaves some of Canada's most spectacular mountain scenery and has three summits, each over a mile high. The most impressive is Highwood Pass, 90 miles north of Coleman. At 7,238 feet it is the highest piece of engineered road in Canada. Snow usually stays until the end of June and can return in late September. Even in midsummer patches lie in the shade of stunted larch and pine. Another impressive piece of geography is some 25 miles north of Coleman. Here is the Livingstone Range where the Oldman River flows through what seems a solid wall of rock. A noticeable feature is that the mountains along the route are different from those flanking other thoroughfares in the Rockies. Some are gray, some are red, while some have whorls resembling gigantic fingerprints over 1,000 feet high. Still others are criss-crossed by massive crevices, vivid evidence of the cataclysmic upheaval which led to the birth of the Rocky Mountains some 75 million years ago.

The treasure of the route is Kananaskis Provincial Park. Here the Alberta government has spent millions of dollars to create a magnificent outdoor playground amidst some 90 square miles of glaciers, lakes, streams and mountain meadows. There are hundreds of campsites with fireplaces, boat launching facilities and hiking trails. The region is also popular in winter, with a variety of cross-country ski trails and a chair lift on Fortress Mountain. Kananaskis Village Resort provides world-class facilities and is open all year.

For the Alberta section of the Crowsnest Pass an era ended in 1983 when the last coal mine closed. This mine, operated by Coleman Collieries Limited, at its peak in 1976 employed 725 men. But decreasing demand led to a steady reduction in the work force until only eighty employees were left. When they were laid off an industry that had endured for over eighty years became history.

By contrast, while mining in the Alberta section of the Pass was declining, the B.C. part was booming. Since 1980, for instance, over $1 billion has been invested in coal mines. This investment has dramatically changed coal mining, the coal miners and the communities. The revolution began in 1947 in the Natal-Michel area when Crowsnest Industries began strip mining for coal. With this system there are no underground tunnels. The overburden is stripped off the coal seams and the coal extracted with massive machines and hauled away by equally massive 240-ton trucks.

While the 240-ton trucks are huge, they are dwarfed by one vehicle called the Terex Titan. It has a locomotive engine which develops 3,300 horsepower and rear wheels powered by electric motors which could supply 3,200 homes with electricity. Its box can hold two Greyhound buses and two pick-ups and loaded it weighs 1 million pounds. In addition to being the largest truck in the world and the only one of its kind, the Titan has an appetite to match its name since it uses up to 550 gallons of diesel fuel every eight hours. After several years, however, it was retired because of the cost of upkeep. It is still visible during tours of the mine.

But while the Titan with its one million pounds was impressive, so is the size of the coal field. One firm alone estimates its reserves at seven billion tons. The technology used today in extracting this coal has made the traditional pick and shovel museum pieces.

At Westar's Balmer operation near Sparwood is Canada's largest open pit mine. It is 5 miles long with nearly 50 miles of road around it. The coal is covered with shale and sandstone overburden ranging from a few feet to upwards of 1,000 and for every ton of coal mined, up to 13 tons of debris must be removed. To remove this overburden the modern miner drills some 250 holes, each over 50 feet deep. They are then filled with over 300,000 pounds of explosives. The resulting blast loosens 300,000 yards of over-burden which is hauled away. Bulldozers then break up the coal which is in a seam up to 50 feet thick, then the massive trucks and a conveyer haul it to a central breaker system. Here it is crushed then transported by another conveyor through a 5,000-foot tunnel to massive coal silos.

But the coal is not yet ready for the modern market. It must, for one thing, be washed. This process is described in a Westar brochure: "During the preparation process, raw coal is conveyed from the storage silos to the wash plant and screened to remove debris. Coal larger than one centimetre (not quite one-half inch) in diameter is washed in heavy media vessels and delivered firectly to the clean coal silos. Finer coal is screened in two sizes for washing by a separate process. After washing, the two size fractions are recombined and conveyed to a thermal dryer to reduce the mositure content. From the dryer, the coal is conveyed to clean silos to await loading onto unit trains.

"At the load-out area, computerized measuring equipment ensures that each car is loaded to its capacity of approximately 92 tons. At the same time, a latex emulsion is sprayed over each full carload to prevent dust from escaping druing the trip to the coast."

The unit trains the brochure mentions were built especially for carrying coal. Each hauls about 10,000 tons and is well over a mile long. The coal cars are never uncoupled. Loading the 111 cars of each unit train is done while the cars pass under the loading facility at one-half mile an hour. Near Vancouver they are unloaded at Roberts Bank, one of the largest and most effective bulk coal terminals in the world.

The massive development of the coal fields has created new communities and resulted in two of the originals vanishing. They were Natal-Michel, bulldozed and burned, their residents moving to Sparwood a few miles west. Sparwood, designed to provide a pleasing life style in con-

The Crowsnest, lowest of any pass through the Rocky Mountains.

trast to the drabness of Natal-Michel, has gorwn into a community of 4,500. It offers a variety of visitor services and has an excellent Chamber of Commerce Information Centre just off Highway 3. Outside the Centre is an impressive wooden statue of a miner which was carved with a chain saw. It commemorates all of the region's miners, its model the late Stanley Wasiewicz who was a pick and shovel miner for over seventy years. In addition, murals depicting the bygone era of mining are painted on the walls in downtown Sparwood.

Twenty miles north of Sparwood is Elkford, another community born because of coal development. It has a population of 4,000 and visitor services which include accommodation and a Municipal Campground with sixty sites and showers, washrooms, fire pits and sani-station. It is the centre for a huge mining operation by Fording Coal.

Visitors interested in seeing an open pit mine can do so in July and August when Westar conducts tours of its Balmer operation with its 5-mile-long open pit and Terex Titan truck. For tour information and reservations check with the Sparwood Chamber of Commerce Information Centre. Phone (604) 425-2423. (In the off season group tours for twenty or more people are available.)

In addition to the coal mine tour, visitors will find other attractions from fishing to camping, golfing to admiring the Rocky Mountain scenery. To serve visitors there are a wide range of business places from deluxe motels to government campgrounds, modern ski facilities to shopping centers.

The Crowsnest Pass in Alberta-B.C. has been in the past buffeted harshly by fate. Those days are history. The region today is optimistic and prosperous. While coal remains king, visitors will find the welcome mat at all communities along this 60-mile-long ribbon of pavement through the Rocky Mountains.

A selection of other *HERITAGE HOUSE* titles:

The PIONEER DAYS IN BRITISH COLUMBIA Series
Every article is true, many written or narrated by those who, 100 or more years ago, lived the experiences they relate. Each volume contains 160 pages in large format magazine size (8½ x 11"), four-color covers, some 60,000 words of text and over 200 historical photos, many published for the first time.

A continuing Canadian best seller in four volumes which have sold over 75,000 copies. Each volume, $11.95

WHITE SLAVES OF THE NOOTKA
On March 22, 1803, while anchored in Nootka Sound on the West Coast of Vancouver Island, the *Boston* was attacked by "friendly" Nootka Indians. Twenty-five of her 27 crew were massacred, their heads "arranged in a line" for survivor John Jewitt to identify. Jewitt and another survivor became 2 of 50 slaves owned by Chief Maquina, never knowing what would come first — rescue or death.

The account of their ordeal, published in 1815, remains remarkably popular. New Western Canadian edition, well illustrated. 128 pages. $9.95

THE DEATH OF ALBERT JOHNSON: Mad Trapper of Rat River
Albert Johnson in 1932 triggered the greatest manhunt in Canada's Arctic history. In blizzards and numbing cold he was involved in four shoot-outs, killing one policeman and gravely wounding two other men before being shot to death.

This revised, enlarged edition includes photos taken by "Wop" May, the legendary bush pilot whose flying skill saved two lives during the manhunt. Another Canadian best seller. $7.95

OUTLAWS AND LAWMEN OF WESTERN CANADA
These true police cases prove that our history was anything but dull. Chapters in 160-page Volume Three, for instance, include Saskatchewan's Midnight Massacre, The Yukon's Christmas Day Assassins, When Guns Blazed at Banff, and Boone Helm — The Murdering Cannibal.

Each of the three volumes in this Canadian best seller series is well illustrated with maps and photos and four-color photos on the covers. Volume One, $8.95; Volume Two, $8.95; Volume Three, $9.95

B.C. PROVINCIAL POLICE STORIES: Mystery and Murder
from the Files of Western Canada's First Lawmen
The B.C. Police, born in 1858, were the first lawmen in Western Canada. During their 90 years of service they established a reputation as one of the most progressive police forces in North America. All cases in this best selling title are reconstructed from archives and police files by ex-Deputy Commissioner Cecil Clark who served on the force for 35 years.

Volume One: 16 chapters, many photos, 128 pages. $8.95
Volume Two: 22 chapters, many photos, 144 pages. $9.95

B.C. BACKROADS
This best selling series contains complete information from Vancouver through the Fraser Canyon to Cache Creek, east to Kamloops country and north to the Cariboo. Also from Vancouver to Bridge River-Lillooet via Whistler. Each book contains mile-by-mile route mileage, history, fishing holes, wildlife, maps and photos.

Volume One — Garibaldi to Bridge River Country-Lillooet. $9.95
Volume Three — Junction Country: Boston Bar to Clinton. $9.95
Thompson-Cariboo: Highways, byways, backroads. $5.95

An Explorer's Guide: MARINE PARKS OF B.C.

To tens of thousands of boaters, B.C.'s Marine Parks are as welcome and convenient as their popular highway equivalents. This guide includes anchorages and onshore facilities, trails, picnic areas, campsites, history and other information. In addition, it is profusely illustrated with color and black and white photos, maps and charts.

Informative reading for boat owners from runabouts to cabin cruisers.
200 pages. $12.95

GO FISHING WITH THESE BEST SELLING TITLES

HOW TO CATCH SALMON — BASIC FUNDAMENTALS

The most popular salmon book ever written. Information on trolling, rigging tackle, most productive lures, proper depths, salmon habits, how to play and net your fish, downriggers, where to find fish.

Sales over 120,000. 176 pages. $5.95

HOW TO CATCH SALMON — ADVANCED TECHNIQUES

The most comprehensive advanced salmon fishing book available. Over 200 pages crammed full of how-to tips and easy-to-follow diagrams. Covers all popular salmon fishing methods: mooching, trolling with bait, spoons and plugs, catching giant chinook, and much more.

A continuing best seller. 192 pages. $11.95

HOW TO CATCH CRABS: How popular is this book? This is the 11th printing, with sales over 90,000. $4.95

HOW TO CATCH BOTTOMFISH: Revised and expanded. $4.95

HOW TO CATCH SHELLFISH: Updated 4th printing. 144 pages. $3.95

HOW TO CATCH TROUT by Lee Straight, one of Canada's top outdoorsmen. 144 pages. $5.95

HOW TO COOK YOUR CATCH: Cooking seafood on the boat, in a camper or at the cabin. 8th printing. 192 pages. $4.95

FLY FISH THE TROUT LAKES

with Jack Shaw

Professional outdoor writers describe the author as a man "who can come away regularly with a string when everyone else has been skunked." In this book, he shares over 40 years of studying, raising and photographing all forms of lake insects and the behaviour of fish to them.

Written in an easy-to-follow style. 96 pages. $7.95

A CUTTHROAT COLLECTION: B.C. experts pool their knowledge and experience to unravel the mysteries and methods of catching this elusive fish. $5.95

SALMON FISHING BRITISH COLUMBIA: Volumes One and Two

Since B.C. has some 7,000 miles of coastline, a problem to its 400,000 salmon anglers is where to fish. These books offer a solution. Volume One includes over 100 popular fishing holes around Vancouver Island. Volume Two covers the Mainland Coast from Vancouver to Jervis Inlet. Both include maps, gear to use, best times, lures and a tackle box full of other information.

Volume One — Vancouver Island. $9.95
Volume Two — Mainland Coast: Vancouver to Jervis Inlet. $11.95

Heritage House books are sold throughout Western Canada. If not available at your bookstore you may order direct from Heritage House, Box 1228, Station A, Surrey, B.C. V3S 2B3. Payment can be by cheque or money order but add 7 per cent for the much hated GST. Books are shipped postpaid.